Men-at-Arms • 506

Roman Army Units in the Western Provinces (1)

31 BC–AD 195

Raffaele D'Amato • Illustrated by Raffaele Ruggeri

Series editor Martin Windrow

First published in Great Britain in 2016 by Osprey Publishing,
PO Box 883, Oxford, OX1 9PL, UK
1385 Broadway, 5th Floor, New York, NY 10018, USA
E-mail: info@ospreypublishing.com

Osprey Publishing, part of Bloomsbury Publishing Plc

A CIP catalogue record for this book is available from the British Library

Print ISBN: 978 1 4728 1537 8
PDF ebook ISBN: 978 1 4728 1538 5
ePub ebook ISBN: 978 1 4728 1539 2

Editor: Martin Windrow
Index by Mark Swift
Map by JB Illustrations
Typeset in Helvetica Neue and ITC New Baskerville

Originated by PDQ Media, Bungay, UK
Printed in China through Worldprint Ltd

16 17 18 19 20   10 9 8 7 6 5 4 3 2 1

Osprey Publishing supports the Woodland Trust, the UK's leading woodland
conservation charity. Between 2014 and 2018 our donations will be spent on
their Centenary Woods project in the UK.

www.ospreypublishing.com

Dedication

To my dear friend Graham Sumner, who believes,
as I do, in the glory that was Rome

Acknowledgements

My special thanks to Dr Michel Feugère, whose provision of illustrations has
enriched this first book in a planned series on Roman units throughout the
Provinces. As always, I am indebted to Prof Livio Zerbini of Ferrara University
for his generous assistance in obtaining permission from different museums
and institutions for me to study and photograph relevant material, particularly
the case of the Museo Archeologico Nazionale di Aquileia, where I am also
indebted to Dr Luigi Fozzati. My gratitude also to Dr Ivan Radman-Livaja for
important photos of the Siscia specimens, and to Dr Maratier Bertrand and Dr
Sarah Hess for photos of the rare sculptures in the Musée Archéologique de
Saintes. I wish to record special thanks to Dr Stefano Izzo, and to Dr Cezary
Wyszynski, for courteous access to their precious photographic archives.

Further gratitude for photographic assistance goes to the Musée Lapidaire de
la Ville de Narbonne; the Musée Gallo-Romaine de Fourvière at Lyon; the
Musée de Antiquité National Saint Germain en Laye; the Musée Rolin d'Autun;
the Musée de Saint Germain-de-Près; the Museo di Antichità di Torino; the
Museo Civico of Cuneo; the Museo Archeologico Nazionale Sanna di Sassari;
the Museo della Civiltà Romana; the British Museum; the Grosvenor Museum
Chester; Carleon Museum; the National Archaeological Museum of Rabat,
Morocco; the Archaeological Museums of Cherchell and of Hyppone (Annaba)
Algeria; the Soprintendenza speciale per Pompeii, Ercolano and Stabia; the
Brugg Museum; the Museum of Aquincum (Budapest); the Römisch-
Germanisches Zentralmuseum, Mainz; Worms Museum; the Limes Museum,
Aalen; the Städtischle Kunstsammlungen; the Archäologische Staatssammlung
München; the Römisches Museum, Augsburg; the Zemaljski Museum, Sarajevo
and the Museos Arqueologico de Granada, de Cordoba and de Tarragona.

As always, I must record my sincere thanks to Dr Andrea Salimbeti and
Dr Andrei Negin, for their meticulous drawings and their patient and
valued help in collecting illustrative material, searching the sources, and
assisting in my various travels. My dear friend Massimo Bizzarri has also been of
great assistance in my research. Last but not least, I am deeply grateful to my
friend and illustrator Raffaele Ruggeri for his splendid new set of colour plates.

Artist's Note

ROMAN ARMY UNITS IN THE WESTERN PROVINCES (1)

31 BC–AD 195

INTRODUCTION

The military history of the Roman provinces under the Principate (Empire) has already received much attention from historians and archaeologists, but there are still plentiful grounds for discussion about the appearance of the Roman soldiers stationed in them. A general idea of standardized Roman equipment has persisted until recent years, but this must now be revisited in view of the variety of archaeological finds related to the Roman legions and auxiliary troops. While a general degree of similarity between the different bodies of troops must be recognized, the analysis of particular finds, as well as of the artistic and literary sources, shows variations in the equipment of the troops based in different regions.

On the subject of the iconography, the present author believes that we should also revise another old conception: that the representations of military equipment are simply a matter of 'artistic conventions'. We can surely imagine that those who produced artworks in both the central empire and the frontier regions had examples of Roman *milites* before their eyes on a regular basis, and were aware of differences in their appearance (particularly when a dead man's heirs were commissioning his funerary monument).[1] Despite the limitations imposed by techniques – carving, fresco and mosaics – and by the artisans' individual skills, the relative accuracy with which craftsmen depicted Roman soldiers is often confirmed by archaeological finds from the relevant provinces.

One particular aspect that arises from the iconography is the apparent use of protective elements made from organic materials such as leather, linen and felt. Close examination suggests that an assumption by scholars that metallic armour must always have been preferred, for its supposedly superior protective qualities, cannot go unchallenged.

The units of non-citizen infantry and cavalry supporting the legions were generally called *auxilia*. These were systematically organized under Augustus by recruitment in the provinces, and from the reign of Claudius (AD 41–54) Roman citizenship began to be extensively awarded to provincials, especially Celts and Easterners. To acquire this valuable status many subjects of the Empire chose a military career, which earned citizenship for the family of the retired *auxiliaris*. Auxiliaries were generally more lightly armed than the legionaries, or constituted units with particular weaponry according to regional traditions. Most monuments to auxiliaries of the 1st and 2nd centuries AD suggest a high standard of equipment, partly because of a general Roman military tendency towards uniformity. However, in many

The cold stare of the mask from a Roman cavalry helmet, mid-1st century AD, recovered at Volubilis in Mauretania Tingitana. Such masks and complete masked helmets have been found all over the Empire, from Scotland to Morocco, and – together with silvered items of armour and horse-harness decorations – were mainly designed for the mounted military display 'sports' known as the Hippika Gymnasia. However, the funerary monuments of Longinus of *Ala Petriana* from Hexham Abbey, and of Genialis of *Ala Augusta Vocontiorum* from Cirencester, suggest that they were also worn on the battlefield. (Museum of Rabat, Morocco, ex-Boube-Picot, courtesy the Museum)

---

1   A note on terminology: for simplicity, in this text we use the terms *stele/stelae*, tombstone and gravestone interchangeably, to mean any type of individual funerary monument.

units this was only partially achieved: a wide range of national costumes and weaponry were retained, and these in turn had an influence on standard Roman equipment. In many garrisons (and not only those of mixed *cohortes equitatae*) the presence of infantry troops alongside cavalrymen is attested, which suggests opportunities for an interchange of material culture via the camp workshops. The evidence has long suggested that the previous idea of a rigid division between the armours of the legionary and the auxiliary is exaggerated.

THE WESTERN PROVINCES

Chronology, 2nd century BC to 2nd century AD

146 BC	Destruction of Carthage; creation of *provincia* of Africa in modern Tunisia and coastal Libya.
125–118 BC	Conquest of southern Gaul and creation of province of Gallia Transalpina.
51 BC	Following conquests by Julius Caesar, rest of Gaul receives the status of a Roman province.
27 BC	Octavian Caesar takes titles Augustus and Princeps as, in all but name, the first Emperor.
***c.*19 BC**	Creation of three Spanish provinces: Hispania Baetica (south-central Spain), Lusitania (roughly Extramadura and Portugal south of the river Douro), and Hispania Tarraconensis (the rest of Spain).

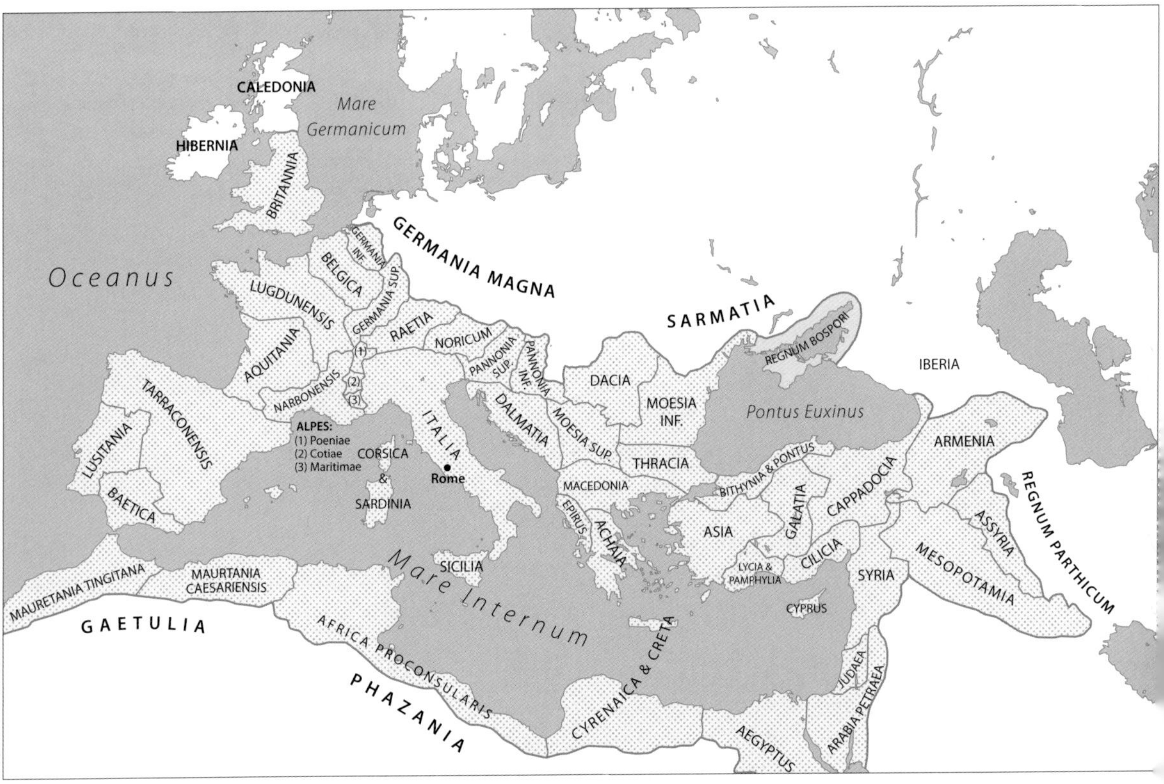

The provinces of the Roman Empire *c.*AD 117 (plus the client Bosporan kingdom north of the Black Sea, *Pontus Euxinus*). Under the Principate (Empire), provinces were classed as either 'imperial' or 'senatorial'. The former were the strategic border provinces, each governed by a *legatus* appointed by the Emperor and more or less heavily garrisoned with legions and auxiliary units. The senatorial provinces were those of the more peaceful inner Empire around the Mediterranean, each governed by a *proconsul* appointed by the senate, with a garrison that less often included legions. Of the territories covered in this book, only Hispania Baetica, Gallia Narbonensis, Italia itself, Sicilia, Corsica-Sardinia and Africa Proconsularis were classed as senatorial. Note that the eastern limits of the provinces covered in this book are Pannonia and Dalmatia. The eastern European provinces of Dacia, Moesia, Thracia, Macedonia, Epirus and Achaia will be included in a future title devoted to units based in the East. (Map by JB Illustrations)

22 BC	Creation of senatorial province of Gallia Narbonensis in modern Languedoc and Provence.
16 BC	Augustus creates three new Gallic provinces: Gallia Belgica (modern N.E. France, Belgium, part of Netherlands and N.W. Germany); Gallia Aquitania (S.W. France); and Gallia Lugdunensis (central France). Noricum (roughly modern Austria) falls under Roman rule.
15–6 BC	Conquest of the Alps; creation of province of Raetia (modern E. & C. Switzerland, S. Bavaria).
12 BC–AD 16	Attempted conquest of Germany and establishment of province of Germania Magna; after the Varus disaster of **AD 9** (battle of Teutoburg Forest) the Roman eastern frontier is consolidated on the Rhine.

AD 7	Augustus divides Italia into 11 administrative *regiones* (Pliny the Elder, *HN*, III, 46).
AD 8–10	Illyricum (roughly modern Albania, Croatia, other parts of former Yugoslavia, E. Austria, W. Hungary, W. Slovakia) is divided into two provinces: Illyricum Superius becomes Dalmatia, and Illyricum Inferius becomes Pannonia.
AD 14	Death of Augustus, succeeded by Tiberius.
AD 37	Death of Tiberius, succeeded by Gaius 'Caligula.'
AD 41	Assassination of Caligula, succeeded by Claudius.
AD 40–44/46	Following incorporation of Numidia into the Roman state, existing North African province is renamed Africa Proconsularis, and two new provinces are created: Mauretania Tingitana (modern N. Morocco) and Mauretania Caesariensis (N. Algeria).
AD 43	Invasion of Britannia begins. During reign of Claudius, Noricum becomes a province.
AD 54	Death of Claudius, succeeded by Nero.
AD 60–61	Boudicca's insurrection in Britannia.
AD 68–69	Suicide of Nero ends Julio-Claudian dynasty; brief successions of Galba, Otho and Vitellius; throne secured by Vespasian, beginning Flavian dynasty.
AD 69–71	Mutinies on German frontier.
AD 72	Active conquest of Wales and northern Britannia resumed.
AD 79	Death of Vespasian, succeeded by Titus.
AD 81	Death of Titus, succeeded by Domitian. Frontiers of Gallic and Germanic provinces extended further east.
AD 83	Chatti War in Germania; building of *limes* to link Upper Rhine and Upper Danube begins.
AD 84	Victory by Agricola in Scotland ends active conquest in Britannia.
AD 90	Creation of provinces of Germania Superior (modern S.W. Germany, W. Switzerland, Jura and Alsace) and Germania Inferior (modern N. Germany west of Rhine, S. Belgium, Luxembourg, S. Netherlands).

1st-century AD fragment of sculpture representing soldiers either of a *Cohors Auxiliaria Mediolanensis*, or legionaries stationed at Aulnay-de-Saintonge in Aquitania. Whatever their exact identity, the combination of a *lorica segmentata* (or at least its shoulder plates) with an embossed cavalry-style helmet of Weiler type raises serious doubts about the supposedly rigid standardization of Roman army equipment. See reconstruction as Plate A2. (Musée Archéologique de Saintes, inv. num. E.1344, photo courtesy the Museum)

AD 96	Assassination of Domitian ends Flavian dynasty; succeeded by Nerva.
AD 98	Death of Nerva, succeeded by Trajan.
AD 103–107	Pannonia is divided into two provinces: Pannonia Superior, with headquarters at Carnuntum (Bad Deutsch-Altenburg, Austria); and Pannonia Inferior, with headquarters at Aquincum (Budapest, Hungary).
*c.***AD 105**	Roman defences in Britannia north of Tyne-Solway line abandoned.
AD 117	Death of Trajan, succeeded by Hadrian.
*c.***AD 122**	Construction of Hadrian's Wall begins between Tyne and Solway.
AD 138	Death of Hadrian, succeeded by Antoninus Pius.
*c.***AD 143**	Defences in northern Britannia advanced to Antonine Wall on Forth-Clyde line.
AD 160–170	Marcomannic Wars on Danube frontier (Raetia, Germania Superior, Pannonia, Noricum)
AD 161	Death of Antoninus, succeeded by Marcus Aurelius. Antonine Wall abandoned.
AD 180	Death of Marcus Aurelius, succeeded by Commodus.
AD 180–184	War in northern Britannia.
AD 192	Commodus assassinated; widespread civil wars.
AD 197	Septimius Severus secures throne.

The army and the frontiers

Distributing land grants to the civil-war veterans, Augustus began reducing the core of the army from 50 to 28 *legiones* to defend the roughly 5,000 miles of the empire's frontiers. With these and auxiliary forces Augustus waged a series of campaigns to complete the pacification of some existing provinces, followed by expansions and conquests. After completing the submission of north-west Spain in 19 BC he left a garrison of four legions in the peninsula, but transferred part of his army to the borders of Germania and Illyricum. In Gaul, however, due to internal threats, the presence of no fewer than 11 legions is attested until AD 16.

At the end of Augustus's reign the army in Germania comprised eight legions (plus, as always, auxiliaries), divided under two headquarters: at Mogontiacum (Mainz), and at the future Colonia Agrippina (Cologne). For both defensive and offensive purposes the legions were concentrated at that

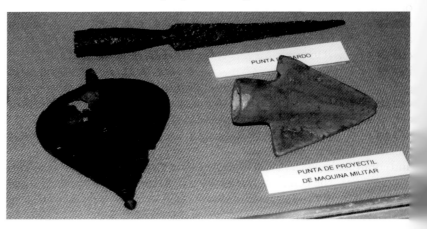

Roman finds from Cordoba in the province of Hispania Baetica, 2nd century AD: a horse-harness pendant (left), and the heads of a *venaculum* (javelin) and a *ballista* bolt. (Museo Arqueologico de Cordoba; author's photo, courtesy the Museum)

ime around Castra Vetera (Xanten) and Mainz, strategic positions
t the confluences of the rivers Lippe, Main and Rhine. Some were
ubsequently transferred to other provinces (see table of known
ocations, pages 13–14).

The empire was expanded to its greatest extent by the soldier-
mperor Trajan (AD 98–117). Thereafter, especially under his
uccessor Hadrian, the frontiers along the Rhine and Danube were
narked by a series of continuous fortifications or *limes* studded with
ermanent garrisons, typically of auxiliaries. From Hadrian onwards
he strategy of the Empire was more usually defensive than offensive.
t that time only four legions were left to defend the Germanic
rovinces, headquartered at Xanten, Bonn, Mainz and Strasbourg
n the Rhine frontier, while six others were stationed along the
Danube in Pannonia and Dalmatia. The Upper Rhine and Upper
Danube were guarded by the Limes Germanicus-Raeticus. After the
Roman consolidation of Britannia the island kept a garrison of three
egions; early in the 2nd century the Limes Britannicus were marked by
Hadrian's Wall, and for a short period in the 150s AD by the more northerly
Antonine Wall. By AD 117 Spain had only one resident legion. The empire's
ongest frontier was that in North-West Africa, where Legio III Augusta was
ased; from the reign of Trajan this border was extended, and defended by
wo lines of garrisons created north and south of the Aurès Mountains.

Sculpture of late 1st-century BC
legionaries on the march, from
Glanum in Gallia Narbonensis.
They wear mail armour, and
helmets resembling Imperial
Gallic Type A under Robinson's
classification; some of these
seem to show the horns of
cornicularii. (Musée Fourviére,
Lyon; photo courtesy Creative
Commons)

DISTRIBUTION OF UNITS

rom the time of Augustus the field army was mainly concentrated on the
rontiers, where rivers such as the Rhine and Danube formed the trace of
he future defensive *limes*. However, permanently garrisoned camps were
naintained further back in the provinces to discourage insurrection, such
s those in Gaul (Arlaines, Aulnay-de-Saintonge, and Mirabeau), and this is
he reason why archaeology in many Western provinces attests a stronger
nilitary presence than scholars once believed. Later, legionary fortresses at
trategic provincial hubs provided back-up for the auxiliary frontier garrisons.
The role of the army was decisive in the process of Romanization throughout
he provinces; many modern European cities were born from Roman
nilitary camps or the *coloniae* established for the settlement of veterans.

The new territories of the Empire were conquered by a professional army
of about 150,000 legionaries, supported by a more or less similar number
of auxiliary troops. These latter were recruited in the different provinces,
nd sometimes in vassal kingdoms as yet outside the empire, whose soldiers
ften specialized in particular military techniques. The size of the army and
ts distribution in the provincial territories was regulated by economic,
geophysical and political factors. The payment of the soldiers' salaries and
he acquisition of their equipment and provisions were met through taxation
nd other sources of income. Conversely, the presence of garrisons was a
najor factor in the economic development of the provinces, where they
created a demand for the supply of large quantities of food, wine, oil, horses
nd draft animals, fodder, leather, metal, pottery, and many other
commodities. The constant demand for these raw materials and products,
specially furnished from the north-eastern provinces along the axes of the
ivers, greatly enriched the provinces themselves.

Head of a *cornicularius*, 2nd
century AD, from Granada in
Hispania Baetica. The applied
horns may originally have been a
decoration for distinguished
service, but the literary sources
indicate that men with this
status served as a hierarchy of
administrative personnel – in the
modern sense, 'chief clerks' – on
the legionary staff. (Granada
Archaeological Museum; author's
photo, courtesy the Museum)

Bronze statuette of a legionary in a *lorica segmentata* (laminated armour) of Sarmatian typology. He wears a *tunica militaris* under a *subarmalis* (under-armour jerkin) of leather or linen fitted with *pteryges* (hanging edge-straps). This *lorica segmentata* is visible on the pedestal of Trajan's Column; very different from the characteristic pattern made of iron strips and plates, the Sarmatian segmented armour, adopted by the Romans during the 2nd century AD, was mainly made of leather, and fastened by hooks on the breast. He also wears *feminalia* (breeches), *caligae*, and a crested helmet of Attic type with a brow band shaped like a diadem. The dress and armour appear typical of the Marcomannic Wars of the 160s–170s AD. (British Museum, ex-Collezione Castellani, inv. GR 1867.5–10.4 (bronze 1611); author's photo, courtesy the Museum)

The legionary camps and fortresses and the auxiliary forts, and the neighbouring townships that grew up to service them, were inhabited by an intermingled military and civilian population: the women and children of auxiliaries and legionaries, merchants, craftsmen, tradespeople, prostitutes, slaves and veterans. Consequently, the particular materials and techniques employed by local artisans influenced the clothing, equipment and accoutrements of legionaries and auxiliaries alike.

Legiones

The army reorganized by Augustus was a professional, long-service regular force formed of both legions and auxiliary units. In modern terms, legions were perhaps large 'infantry brigade groups', *c*.4,920–5,240 strong (Julio-Claudian/Flavian periods), comprising ten infantry cohorts or 'battalions'. At that time the legions were recruited from Roman citizens, mainly Italics, who received a good salary and retirement benefits. Until the 3rd century AD the number of legions varied between 30 and 33, and during these 200 years their ethnic composition gradually changed as many more provincial citizens were enlisted.

The numerical designation of each legion was permanent, and due to the earlier civil wars these were sometimes duplicated, but each legion was also distinguished by an individual name – e.g. Legio I Italica, Legio I Minervia, Legio I Adiutrix, etc. These names had various types of derivation and were often awarded in combinations added successively:

(a) from its formation as the 'twin' of an earlier legion (e.g. Legio XII *Gemina* Pia Fidelis).

(b) from its formation as an 'added' reserve (e.g. Legio II *Adiutrix*).

(c) from the name of a province where it was originally stationed (e.g. Legio IV *Macedonica*).

(d) from an Emperor's dynastic name (e.g. Legio XXX *Ulpia* Victrix, raised by Trajan – Marcus Ulpius Nerva Traianus). Subsequent loyalty to an Emperor was rewarded by adding the suffix *Pia Fidelis* ('Pious and Faithful')

(e) from a god (e.g. Legio XIV Gemina *Martia* Victrix, for Mars).

(f) from an aspect of its earned renown (e.g. Legio IIII Flavia *Felix*, 'Lucky'; Legio VI *Victrix*, 'Victorious'; Legio XXI *Rapax*, 'Rapacious', etc).

(g) from some visible element of equipment (Legio V *Alaudae*, 'the Larks', thought to be named from the two side feathers apparently worn on their helmets).

No names are recorded for Legiones XVII, XVIII and XIX, wiped out under Varus in the Teutoburg Forest disaster of AD 9, and, notoriously, these numbers were never allotted again. Equally, at some point in the 2nd century Legio VIIII Hispana disappeared from the army list (last attested in AD 131, it was absent from lists in the reign of Septimius Severus, AD 193–211).

The legions did not always serve as complete formations. Temporary task forces were often assembled ad hoc with detachments from the legions, to meet a crisis or to undertake offensive missions. These detachments were called *vexillationes* (derived from *vexillum*, 'flag'), and also included attached auxiliary troops. While varying in size, such vexillations might typically number about 1,000 infantrymen and 500 cavalrymen.

From 13 BC until the mid-1st century AD, after serving for 16 years, legionary veterans were transferred into a unit called the *vexillum veteranorum* for a further four years' service (the enlistment term was increased to 25 years under Vespasian). With a strength of about 500 men and their own officers, they might be attached to the legion or deployed for independent duties. For example, such veterans were sent to defend Raetia against the Suebi in AD 14 (Tac. *Ann.*, I, 44), and defeated the Numidian rebel Tacfarinas in AD 20 (Tac. *Ann.*, III, 21).

Auxilia

The permanently embodied auxiliary units had evolved from the groups of *socii* ('allies') of the Consular period. Usually the *auxilia* were recruited inside the provinces from various races of *peregrini* (non-citizens), and enlisted to serve some for 25 years; upon their discharge they and their descendants received Roman citizenship, confirmed (at least from the Claudian period) by a bronze diploma. Some auxiliaries were *Latini*, Italics enjoying certain legal rights short of full citizenship; a few were *Ingenui*, freed slaves (Cheesman, 65, 1914); one Italian unit raised by Augustus in Campania, Cohors I Campanorum Voluntaria, was of mixed citizens and freedmen; some individual provincial citizens enlisted, and some units were raised from citizens, e.g. Cohors I Civium Romanorum Equitata. Again, inscriptions show that some cohorts were composed of veterans. Initially auxiliary units were not fully trusted (especially after the Varus disaster), and when deployed in field armies they remained under the operational authority of a *legatus legionis*. As time passed, however, they acquired greater autonomy, probably due to their dispersion in permanent frontier garrisons, and their organization underwent various changes.

The auxiliary cavalry *alae* and infantry *cohortes* were also numbered and initially named after the relevant province, e.g. Cohors VII Lusitanorum ('Seventh Cohort of Lusitanians'). However, they were more often named from a specific tribal group within a province (e.g. Arevaci, Astures, Bracari or Bracaraugustani, Cantabri, Gallaeci, Luggones, Varduli, Vascones, Vettones, etc, all from Spain). A very few units bore instead the name of their first commander, e.g. the Ala Petriana. Part-mounted cohorts with integral cavalry squadrons were identified by *equitata* in their title, and some titles referred to particular weapons (e.g. Sagittariorum 'archers', or Gaesatorum 'spearmen').

Some units bore the dynastic name of the Emperor who raised them (i.e. Augusta; Flavia for Vespasian and his sons; Ulpia for Trajan; Aelia for Hadrian; and Aurelia for Antoninus Pius, Marcus Aurelius and Commodus). Like the legions, many were also given additional honorific titles; these might indicate collective decorations, e.g. a Cohors Torquata, or a collective award of citizenship, e.g. Cohors II Nerviorum Civium Romanorum. One striking example of a 'compound' title for a battle-hardened unit, which we find on the Danube frontier during

1st–2nd century AD helmet brow bands recovered at Amerongen, Germania Inferior, and in Gallia Lugdunensis, confirming the employment of Attic-type helmets in the northern provinces. The *imago* or portrait of the Emperor on the decorated example can be identified as either Nerva or Trajan. (Rijkmuseum Kam., Nijmegen, & Rijkmuseum Van Oudmeden, Leiden; drawings by Andrei Negin)

Statuette of a Gallo-Roman cavalryman from a bronze harness breast decoration, recovered at Orange in Gallia Narbonensis. The helmet is of Attic style, with a deep, decorated brow band. (Musée de Saint Germain-de-Près; photo courtesy Dr Cezary Wyszynski)

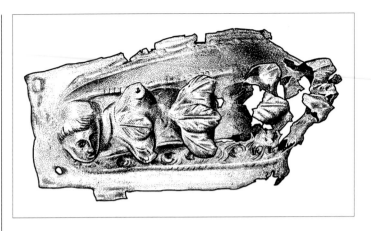

Decorated brow band of an Attic-type Roman helmet recovered from the river Waal at Nijmegen, Germania Inferior. (Rijkmuseum Kam., Nijmegen; drawing by Andrei Negin)

Trajan's reign, is Cohors I Brittonum Ulpia Torquata Pia Fidelis Milliaria Civium Romanorum; this might b translated as 'Trajan's Own Decorate and Loyal First British Thousand Strong Battalion awarded Roma Citizenship'.

Units might be stationed in th provinces where they were recruited o often, on another frontier entirely. Th name of a cohort might even refer t the province in which it was statione rather than to the original ethnicity c the soldiers who had formed it. Agai like legions, auxiliary units often remained in one station for generation and local recruiting quickly diluted their ethnic identity. The historia Mommsen proposed that auxiliary units were recruited only in the imperia provinces, but newly discovered inscriptions, for instance from Los Corrale in Baetica, show that in the second half of the 2nd century AD they wer also being raised in senatorial provinces.

Some auxiliary units were provincial or municipal militias raised to mec particular local threats, such as the Cohors Servia Juvenalis at Castulo i Spain in AD 41–63 (CIL II, 3272), and the Cohors Baetica raised to confror Moorish incursions from Africa in AD 173. These remained embodied fc however long the threat was recognized, commanded by local leaders c equestrian rank, but were deployed only in their own province.

Numeri

During the Principate separate units of *sagittarii* (archers) were created These were examples of the semi-barbarian units called *numeri*, raised i the east of the empire but also deployed on the western frontiers. Suc units, also called *symmacharii*, were enlisted from border peoples wh fought under the command of their own tribal leaders. They might b designated according to their ethnicity and/or their special armament (e.g Numerus Delmatorum, Numerus Sagittariorum). Troops termed *lev armaturae* (light armoured infantry) served on provincial borders under th command of legionary officers seconded to them (CIL X, 3044, 4868, 6098 e.g., CIL X, 3044 mentions Sextus Pedius, Prefect of Raetii and Vindolicii

Praetoriani, Equites Singulares, Germani Corporis Custodes and Evocati Augusti

Cassius Dio writes (LV, 24) of the troops in Italy: 'Then there were th bodyguards, ten thousand in number and organized in ten divisions, an the watchmen of the city, six thousand in number and organized in fou divisions; and there were also picked foreign horsemen, who were give the name of Batavians, after the island of Batavia in the Rhine... I canno however, give their exact number any more than I can that of the *Evocat* Augustus began to make a practice of employing these last-named from th time when he recalled into service against Antony the troops who ha served with his father [Julius Caesar, his adoptive father], and he maintaine them afterwards; they constitute even now a special corps, and carry rod like the centurions…'.

The *praetoriani* constituted the 'Imperial Guard', together with (until the time of Galba) the *Germani corporis custodes*, the *equites singulares Augusti* and the *evocati Augusti*. Augustus formed nine elite Praetorian cohorts (later increased to ten); each cohort comprised 500–1,000 men, paid three times as much as the regular troops and with a reduced term of service (16 years). This Praetorian Guard was based in and around Rome, and constituted – together with the other Imperial bodyguards, plus the *Urbaniciani* and the *Vigiles* – the only armed force in Italy (where they were mainly recruited until the reign of Septimius Severus). They came under the command of a special officer of equestrian rank, the *praefectus praetorii*.

The *equites singulares Augusti* or *Armigeri* (Prop., *El.*, III, 8) were an *ala milliaria* of picked cavalrymen, separate from the praetorians and drawn from different units. The *Germani corporis custodes* (German Bodyguards) were a cohort of ferocious Batavi, considered more reliably loyal than the other guards; upon their enlistment they were granted, if they did not already hold it, Roman citizenship.

The *evocati Augusti* were created by Augustus, as attested by Cassius Dio (see above) and by inscriptions (CIL VI, 2789). They were recruited from the troops based in Rome, i.e. especially the praetorians, the *urbaniciani* (CIL VI, 2384, 2803, 2870), and the marines of the *classis Misenatis*, of which a detachment was based in Rome (CIL X, 3417). While under the command of the Praetorian Prefect (CIL VI, 2009), they did not constitute an organized military unit, but rather a category of personnel who were reserved for duties of particular importance (CIL III, 586; VI, 2725, 2733, 2839, 5840; VII, 257; X, 3732; XI, 19). While of inferior rank to those *primipilares* who were attached to the Emperor's staff, they camped with them in the *castrum* (Pseudo-Hyg., *De Mun. Castr.*, VI). Others were attached to the legions across the Roman world, performing missions of trust.

Head of Ares from Villa Torlonia, Rome, 1st century AD. Again, note the Attic diadem-shaped brow band of the helmet, which seems to have been popular among elite soldiers such as Imperial guardsmen; this sculpture probably echoes contemporary Praetorian equipment, and contributes to our reconstruction as Plate H3. (Drawing courtesy Andrei Negin)

2nd-century AD mosaic from a villa near Sassari in Sardinia, representing the shields of a cohort of *Vigiles*. (Museo Archeologico Nazionale Sanna, Sassari; author's photo, courtesy the Museum)

Dagger and scabbard decorated in silver and enamel, first half/ middle 1st century AD, from Al#riot in Belgica. (Mus#e Denon, Chalon-sur-Sa#ne, courtesy Prof Michel Feug#re)

Urbaniciani and Vigiles

The *urbaniciani* were soldiers of the 'city cohorts', under the comman of a senator of consular rank who headed the *praefectura urbana*. The were divided into four very large 1,500-man cohorts with numeric designations following on from those of the praetorian cohorts (i. initially X, XI, XII and XIII). Each was commanded by a tribune chose from among former legionary *primipilares*. In the 2nd century AD the passed from the command of an Urban Prefect to that of the Praetoria Prefect. During the first two centuries of the Principate the garrison Lugdunum (Lyon) included a rotating 500-man urban cohort detache from Rome's garrison; the sources mention Cohortes XIII, XIV, XV and XVIII, and I Flavia Urbana.

In addition to these security troops, from AD 6 seven cohorts of *vigil* ('watchmen') were raised for police and fire-watching duties. They wer under the control of a *praefectus vigilum* (Watch Prefect), and each wa led by a *tribunus*, a *princeps* and seven centurions. The Watch Prefect an all the junior officers were drawn from regular army units, so we ma suppose that they kept their former uniforms.

Table of identified units, locations and dates

Note: No list can pretend to be fully comprehensive. Fragmentary inscriptions, varying order of words, inconsistent spellings and successive changes of title make some identifications of auxiliary units speculative, and some duplications inevitable (some legions were also renamed for political reasons, e.g. after the death of the hated Domitian). Over time, some numeral styles changed – e.g. 'IIII' and 'IV', 'VIIII' and 'IX'. In the sources not all vexillations are specifically identified as such, which explains apparently contradictory locations/dates for various legions. Unless specifically noted as a *cohors* or *ala milliaria*, listed auxiliary units are *quingenaria* – though that word is also included in unit titles from some sources. Where locations are listed, the first mention gives the Roman name, followed by (the modern name if known), followed by the province.

Abbreviations used: CR = *Civium Romanorum*; eq. = *equitata*;

mill. = *milliaria*; ped. = *peditata*;

PF = *Pia Fidelis*; and quin. = *quingenaria*.

Legiones:

Unit	Location	Date or reign
Legio I Italica	Gallia	March/April AD 68
	Lugdunum (Lyon), Gallia Lugdunensis	AD 69
	Bedriacum (Calvatone), Italia	AD 69
Legio I Minervia	Bonna (Bonn), Germania Inferior	1st–2nd century AD
	Gallia Belgica	AD 173
Legio I Minervia (vexillatio)	Lugdunum, G. Lugdunensis	AD 198–200
Legio I Adiutrix	Bedriacum, Italia	AD 69
	Hispania	AD 69–88
	Mogontiacum (Mainz), Germania Inferior	AD 88–104
	Pannonia	1st–2nd century AD
	Brigetio (Szöny), Pannonia	from AD 114/118
Legio I Adiutrix (vexillatio)	Mursa (Osijek), Dalmatia	2nd–3rd century AD
Legio II Adiutrix	Germania	AD 71
	Lindum (Lincoln), Britannia	1st century AD
	Deva (Chester), Britannia	from AD 76/79
	Danube frontier	AD 90
	Acumincum (Stari Slankamen), Pannonia	end 1st century AD
	Aquincum (Budapest), Pannonia	1st–3rd century AD
	Laugaricio, Limes Pannonicus	AD 179

Legio II Adiutrix (vexillatio)	Mursa, Dalmatia	2nd–3rd century AD
Legio II Augusta	Argentoratum (Strasbourg), Germania Superior	AD 17–43
	Britannia	AD 43
	Glevum (Gloucester), Britannia	AD 66–74
	Isca Silurum (Caerleon), Britannia	AD 74–274
Legio III Augusta	Thugga, Africa Proconsularis	30 BC–AD 24
	Lambaesis, Mauretania Caesariensis	AD 37–3rd century
Legio III Italica	Thamugadi (Timgad), Mauretania Caesariensis	AD 100
	Abusina (Kastell Eining), Raetia	AD 172
	Castra Regina (Regensburg), Germania Superior	AD 179
Legio IV	(under consuls Hirtius and Pansa) Italia	43 BC
Legio IV (veterans)	Sora, Italia	31–27 BC
Legio IIII Macedonica	Pisoraca (Herrera de Pisuerga), Hispania Tarraconensis	28 BC–AD 70
	Colonia Caesaraugusta (Zaragoza), H. Tarraconensis	1st century AD
	Mogontiacum, Germ. Inf.	AD 41–69
Legio IIII Flavia Felix	Burnum (Kistanje), Dalmatia	late 1st century AD
Legio IIII Scytica	Illyrian Wars	AD 6–9
	Germania	AD 49
Legio V Alaudae	Gallia Aquitania	AD 14
	Germania Inferior	AD 14–69
	Italia	AD 69
Legio VI Victrix	Legio (Léon), Hispania Tarraconensis	28 BC–AD 70
	Novaesium (Neuss), Germania Inferior	AD 70
	Vetera (Xanten), Germ. Inf.	AD 89
	Britannia	AD 122
	Eboracum (York), Britannia	2nd–3rd century AD
Legio VII	Hispania	65 BC
Legio VII Claudia Pia Fidelis	Tilurium (Trilj), Dalmatia	AD 6–60
Legio VII Gemina	Pannonia	AD 69–74
	Legio, H. Tarraconensis	AD 74–2nd century
	Mirabeau, G. Lugdunensis	AD 69–78
	Argentoratum, Germania Superior	2nd half 1st century AD–2nd century AD
Legio VII Gemina (vexillatio)	Aquae Querquenniae (Porto Quintela), H. Tarraconensis	AD 69–138
Legio VII Gemina (vexillatio)	Italica (Santiponce), Hispania Baetica	2nd half 2nd century AD
Legio VIII Augusta	Britannia	AD 43
	Lugdunum, G. Lugdunensis	AD 197
Legio VIIII Hispana	Sicilia	41 BC
	Siscia (Sisak), Pannonia	AD 7–45
	Longthorpe, Britannia	AD 48–62
	Lindum, Britannia	AD 65
	Eboracum, Britannia	AD 108
Legio VIIII Hispana (vexillatio)	Noviomagus (Nijmegen), Germania Inferior	AD 131
Legio X Gemina	Asturica Augusta (Astorga), Hispania Tarraconensis	28 BC–AD 70
	Petavonium (Rosinos de Vidriales), H. Tarraconensis	28 BC–AD 70
	Noviomagus, Germ. Inf.	AD 69
	Colonia Caesaraugusta (Zaragoza), H. Tarraconensis	1st century AD
Legio X Gemina Pia Fidelis	Aquincum, Pannonia	AD 100 or 104
	Mursa, Dalmatia	AD 102–107
	Vindobona (Vienna), Pannonia	1st–2nd century AD
	Carnuntum (Bad Deutsch-Altenburg), Pannonia	2nd century AD
	Gornioi, Pannonia	2nd–3rd century AD
Legio XI	Gallia	1st century BC
	Italia	42–38 BC
Legio XI Claudia Pia Fidelis	Burnum, Dalmatia	1st century AD
	Vindonissa (Windisch), Germania Superior	AD 69–100
Legio XII	Octodurus (Martigny), Alpes Poeninae	57–56 BC
Legio XIII Gemina	Sicilia	41 BC
	Vindonissa (Brugg), Germania Superior	AD 6–45
	Poetovium, Pannonia	AD 45
Legio XIIII Gemina Martia Victrix	Mogontiacum, Germ. Inf.	from AD 6
	Aunedonnacum (Aulnay-de-Saintonge), Gallia Aquitania	AD 15–43
	Mursella, Pannonia	AD 92–94
	Vindobona, Pannonia	1st–2nd century AD
	Carnuntum, Pannonia	2nd century AD
Legio XIIII GMV (vexillatio)	Ad Flexum, Italia	2nd century AD
Legio XIIII GMV (vexillatio)	Aquincum, Pannonia	2nd century AD
Legio XIIII GMV (vexillatio)	Mursa, Dalmatia	2nd–3rd century AD
Legio XIIII Gemina (vexillatio)	Siscia, Pannonia	AD 93
Legio XIIII Gemina	Siscia	2nd–3rd century AD
Legio XV Apollinaris	Pannonia	AD 6
	Carnuntum, Pannonia	1st–2nd century AD
Legio XV Primigenia	Mogontiacum, Germania Inf.	c.AD 39–43
	Vetera, Germania Inferior	AD 43–70
Legio XVIII	Vetera, Germania Inferior	15 BC–AD 5
	Kalkriese, Germania	AD 9
Legio XIX	Sicilia	41 BC
	Dangestetten, Germania Sup.	15–7 BC
	Aliso (Haltern), Germania Superior	11 BC–AD 16
Legio XX	Hispania Tarraconensis	25–13 BC
	Siscia, Pannonia	AD 6

Legionary organization

The internal organization of a legion differed slightly from time to time or from legion to legion, but the general picture was as follows.

Its infantry strength was c.4,800–6,200 *milites legionis*. Each of 60 *centuriae* normally had 80 men (Josephus, *BJ*, I, 15, 6), but sometimes 100, led by a *centurio* and his junior officers: the *signifer* (standard-bearer – or the *aquilifer* (eagle-bearer), in the First Century of the First Cohort); the *optio* (centurion's deputy); the *cornicen* and *bucinator* (trumpeters); and the *tesserarius* ('officer of the watchword'). A *custos armorum* was a soldier fulfilling armourer's duties; and a *beneficiarius* was a soldier or junior officer acting as a bodyguard or charged by his superior officer with other special tasks, and thus exempted from fatigue duties. The *antesignani*, a term from the Consular period meaning 'those before the standard', are still mentioned in sources of the Imperial period, as are *postsignani*, indicating picked men fighting in front of or behind the standard.

Six centuries normally formed a *cohors* (battalion) of 480–600 men (Pseudo-Hyginus, *De Mun. Castr.*, I, 7, 8, 30). The cohort might alternatively be divided into three *manipuli* each of two centuries, giving the maniple 160–200 men. Ten cohorts formed the legion (Aul. Gell., *Noct. Att.*, XVI, 4, 6); but from the Flavian period the First Cohort was of double size, with 800–1,000 men in five double-size centuries (*De Mun. Castr.*, III). This was led by the very experienced *primus pilus* ('first javelin'), the most senior of all the legion's centurions; however, in the late 1st century AD Josephus writes (*Contra Apionem*, 21, 38) that the First Cohort commander was the *tribunus laticlavius*. This young aristocrat of senatorial family was the senior of the six tribunes who assisted the legionary commander in largely administrative duties; the other five were *tribuni augusticlavi*, of the equestrian social order. The commander himself, usually of senatorial rank, was termed (like the governor of an Imperial province) the *legatus*, because he was 'delegated' by the Emperor (SHA, *Comm.*, VI, 1), and the *tribunus laticlavius* was officially this legate's second-in-command. Below the legate the senior officer with military experience was the *praefectus castrorum*, usually an ex-*primus pilus*; with responsibility for all practical aspects of the legion's duties, he took over command in the absence of the legate and senior tribune.

Each legion also had an integral cavalry unit of about 120 men, employed as scouts and couriers; they were organized in four 32-man *turmae* (squadrons), each *turma* led by a *decurio*. Each cohort of a legion also had perhaps 120 attached *calones* (servants).

For more detail, see Osprey Battle Orders 37, *The Roman Army of the Principate 27 BC–AD 117*.

Legio XX Valeria Victrix	Camulodunum (Colchester), Britannia	AD 43–50
	Deva, Britannia	AD 95–2nd century
Legio XXI Rapax	Vindonissa (Brugg), Germania Superior	AD 45–69
	Mogontiacum, Germania Inf.	AD 70–89
	Mursella, Pannonia	AD 93
Legio XXII Primigenia	Germania Superior	AD 39
	Vindobona, Pannonia	AD 70
	Mogontiacum, Germania Inf.	2nd–3rd century AD
	Lugdunum, G. Lugdunensis	AD 197
Legio XXX Ulpia Victrix Pia Fidelis	Vetera, Germania Inferior	from AD 119 or 122
	Niedermormter, Germania Inferior	AD 197
	Lugdunum, G. Lugdunensis	AD 197
Legio Arabica	Gallia (under D. Clodius Albinus)	AD 193/197

Auxilia & Urbaniciani:

Units of unspecified strength:

Brittones Aurelianenses	Vicus Aurelianus, Germania Superior	AD 200
Desidiates (Dacians)	Dalmatia	1st century AD
Raeti	Castellum Ircavium, Raetia	1st half 1st century AD

Cohortes:

Cohors Auxiliaria (Mediolanensis?)	Mediolanum (Saintes), Gallia Aquitania	1st half 1st century AD
Cohors Baetica	Bergomum, Raetia	2nd half 1st century AD
Cohors (Belgica?)	Mediolanum, G. Aquitania	AD 20–40
Cohors Gallica	–	–
Cohors Hamiorum Sagittariorum	Vercovicium (Housesteads), Britannia	early 2nd century AD
Cohors Maritima	Corduba (Cordoba), Hispania Baetica	1st–2nd century AD
Cohors Orae Maritimae	Tarraco (Tarragona) or Novae Tironum Hispania Tarraconensis	1st–2nd century AD
Cohors Raetorum et Vindelicorum	Mogontiacum, Germania Inferior	Augustus
Cohors Sagittariorum	Italica, Hispania Baetica	2nd half 2nd century AD
Cohors Servia Juvenalis	Castulo (Cazlona), Hispania Baetica	AD 43–63
Cohors prima	Hispania Baetica	–
Cohors I Aelia Brittonum milliaria	Virunum (Magdalensburg), Noricum	2nd half 2nd century AD
Cohors I Aelia Dacorum milliaria	Britannia	2nd–3rd century AD
Cohors I Aelia Gaesorum	Resculum (Bologa), Pannonia	AD 110–115
Cohors I Aelia Hispanorum milliaria equitata	Alauna? (Maryport), Britannia	c.AD 120
Cohors I Aelia Sagittariorum milliaria equitata	Astura, Noricum	Hadrian
	Cannabiaca (Klostenburg), Vindobona, Ala Nova (Schwechat) & Carnuntum, Pannonia	Marcomannic Wars
Cohors I Aelia Singulariorum	Mauretania Caesariensis	2nd century AD
Cohors I Afrorum CR	Britannia	AD 122
Cohors I Alpinorum peditata	Lussorium, Pannonia	2nd half 1st century AD
Cohors I Alpinorum equitata	Sirmium, Pannonia	2nd half 1st century AD
Cohors I eq. Alpinorum quingenaria	Matricus & Vetus Salina (Adony), Pannonia Inferior	1st–2nd century AD
Cohors I Alpinorum peditata quingenaria	Britannia	AD 103
Cohors I Aquitanorum	Caput Thyrsi (Bitti), Sardinia	1st century AD
Cohors I Aquitanorum quin. (I Aquitanorum Biturigium).	Arae Flaviae, (Rottweil), Germania Superior	AD 74, 90, 116 & 134
Cohors I Aquitanorum (I Aquitanorum quin. eq.)	Brocolitia (Carrawburgh), Britannia	2nd century AD
Cohors I Aquitanorum quin. eq. Veterana	Stockstadt am Main, Germania Superior	1st–2nd century AD
Cohors I Asturum	Astura, Noricum	AD 106
Cohors I Asturum equitata	Mainhardt, Germania Sup.	AD 74–82
	Germania Superior	AD 90–134
Cohors I Asturum et Callaecorum	Illyricum	AD 61
	Mauretania Tingitana	AD 109–136
Cohors I Augusta Ituraeorum equitata	Mogontiacum, Germania Inferior	1st century AD
	Brigetio, Pannonia	AD 79–103
Cohors I Baetasiorum CR	Barr Hill, Britannia	1st–2nd century AD
Cohors I Batavorum eq. quin.	Germania Inferior	Claudius
Cohors I Batavorum eq. mill.	Pannonia Superior	1st–2nd century AD
Cohors I Bataviorum mill. PF	Pannonia	1st century AD
Cohors I Belgica equitata	Mogontiacum, Germ. Inf.	1st century AD
	Gallia Aquitania	1st century AD
	Dalmatia	2nd century AD
Cohors I Bracaugustanorum	Pannonia	AD 6–9
Cohors I Breucorum CR	Britannia	Hadrian
Cohors I Britannica (or Brittonum)	Pannonia	AD 71
Cohors I Brittonum Aelia milliaria	Faviana (Mautern), Noricum	2nd century AD
Cohors I Brittonum Flavia	Dalmatia	after AD 86
Cohors I Brittonum Ulpia Torquata Pia Fidelis mill. CR	Vetus Salina, Pannonia Inferior	AD 105
Cohors I Caesariensis Aelia milliaria Sagittaria	Pannonia Superior	AD 133
Cohors I Chalcidenorum eq.	Numidia/Mauretania	1st–2nd century AD
Cohors I Campana	Dalmatia	AD 6–9
Cohors I Campanorum Voluntariorum Antonianae	Acumincum, Pannonia Inferior	AD 156
Cohors I Campanorum Voluntariorum CR	Pannonia Inferior	2nd century AD

Cohors I Celtiberorum equitata quingenaria	Mauretania Tingitana	AD 105–109
	Britannia	2nd century AD
Cohors I Classica Aelia	Britannia	AD 158
Cohors I Civium Romanorum equitata	Germania Inferior	c.AD 120
Cohors I Dacorum Aelia milliaria	Britannia	2nd century AD
	Lauriacum (Enns), Noricum	2nd half 2nd century AD
Cohors I Damascenorum Flavia mill. eq. Sagittariorum	Germania Superior	AD 79–134
Cohors I Dardanorum Aurelia	Dalmatia	2nd half 2nd century AD
Cohors I Delmatorum eq.	Bremenium (High Rochester), Britannia	1st–2nd century AD
Cohors I Delmatorum mill.	Uzice, Dalmatia	2nd half 2nd century AD
Cohors I Flavia Urbana	Lugdunum, G. Lugdunensis	AD 69–79
Cohors I Flavia equitata	Numidia/Mauretania	AD 128
Cohors I Frisiavonum quin.	Britannia	1st–3rd century AD
Cohors I Gallica	Pisoraca, H. Tarraconensis	28 BC–AD 70
Cohors I Gallica equitata CR	Aquae Querquenniae, H. Tarraconensis	AD 69–138
Cohors I Gallorum	Gallia Aquitania	Augustus
Cohors I Gaesatorum Aelia milliaria	Crumerum, Pannonia Sup.	AD 161
Cohors I Germanorum Nervia milliaria CR	Germania Superior	AD 82–134
	Britannia	AD 122
Cohors I Hamiorum Sagittariorum	Britannia	AD 43, 125–160
Cohors I Helvetiorum	Böckingen, Limes Raeticus	AD 148
Cohors I Hemesenorum eq. mill. Sagittaria CR	Intercisa, Pannonia Inf.	2nd half 2nd century AD
Cohors I Hispanorum	Remagen, Germ. Inf.	early Trajan
Cohors I Hispanorum eq.	Ardoch, Britannia	AD 82
Cohors I Hispanorum Flavia equitata milliaria	Maryport, Britannia	early Trajan/Hadrian
Cohors I Hispanorum Flavia Ulpia milliaria	Dalmatia	AD 85–86
Cohors I Ituraeorum CR	Mauretania Tingitana	2nd century AD
Cohors I Latobicorum et Varcianorum	Ara Ubiorum, Germ. Inf.	AD 92–152
Cohors I Lemavorum CR	Mauretania Tingitana	2nd century AD
Cohors I Ligurum eq. quin.	Alpes	Augustus
Cohors I Ligurum et Hispanorum	Germania Superior	1st century AD
Cohors I Lingonum equitata	Lanchester, High Rochester & Corbridge, Britannia	mid-2nd century AD
Cohors I Lucensium	Dalmatia	AD 6–9
Cohors I Maurorum milliaria	Ad Mauros (Efferding), Noricum	AD 171
Cohors I Menapiorum	Britannia	AD 122–124
Cohors I Montanorum	Dalmatia	AD 6–9
	Noricum & Pannonia	AD 57–85
Cohors I Montanorum CR quin	Pannonia Inferior	1st–2nd century AD
Cohors I Morinorum	Britannia	2nd century AD
Cohors I Musulamiorum Flavia	Numidia/Mauretania	Trajan
Cohors I Nerviorum Augusta	Caer Gai, Britannia	1st–2nd century AD
Cohors I Pannoniorum quingenaria	Bingen am Rhein, Germania Superior	AD 41–54
Cohors I Pannoniorum	Mauretania Caesariensis	2nd century AD
Cohors I Pannoniorum Ulpia milliaria equitata	Gerulata (Rusovce), Pannonia Superior	2nd century AD
Cohors I Pannoniorum et Delmatarum equitata CR	Germania Inferior	2nd century AD
Cohors I Pasinatum Aurelia Nova	Dalmatia	2nd half 2nd century AD
Cohors I Raetorum quin.	Raetia	2nd century AD
	Katwijik (Germania Sup.) Ara Ubiorum (Germ. Inf.)	2nd half 2nd century AD
Cohors I Sacorum Aurelia Nova	Kosmaj (Guberecvi), Dalmatia	2nd half 2nd century AD
Cohors I Septima Belgarum	Vicus Aurelianus (Öhringen), Germania Superior	AD 200
Cohors I Sequanorum et Rauracorum eq. quin.	Germania Superior	2nd century AD
Cohors I Sugambrorum Claudia ironum Veterana	Gallia Belgica	1st century AD
Cohors I Sunicorum/Sunucorum quin.	Germania Inferior	AD 69
	Britannia	2nd century AD
Cohors I Thracum equitata CR	Germania	1st century AD
	Hadrian's Wall, Britannia	2nd century AD
(Cohors I Thracum CR eq.)	Pannonia	2nd century AD
Cohors I Treverorum eq.	Zugmantel, Germania Sup.	mid-2nd century AD
Cohors I Tungrorum mill.	Germania Inferior	1st–2nd century AD
	Brocolitia (Chesterholm), Britannia	Hadrian
	Noricum	AD 122–124
	Vindolanda, Britannia	AD 146
Cohors I Ubiorum equitata	Noricum	1st century AD
Cohors I Ulpia Brittonum	Resculum, Pannonia	early 1st century AD
Cohors I Ulpia Traiana Cugernorum CR	Britannia	2nd–3rd century AD
Cohors I Ulpia Traiana Campestris Voluntariorum	Mursa, Dalmatia	2nd–3rd century AD
Cohors I Vangionum milliaria equitata	Condercum (Benwell), Britannia	mid-2nd century AD
Cohors I fida Vardullorum milliaria equitata CR	Castlecary, Britannia	mid-2nd century AD
Cohors I Vasconum eq. CR	Hispania	AD 68
	Germania	AD 69
	Britannia	2nd century AD
Cohors I Vindelicorum	Ara Ubiorum, Germania Inf.	1st–2nd century AD

Auxiliary organization

Auxiliaries formed units of c.480–600 men: cavalry *alae* (with 16 *turmae* of 32 men); infantry *cohortes* (with 6 *centuriae* of 80 men); or mixed *cohortes equitatae*, with 6 centuries of *pedites* plus 4 squadrons of *equites*. This so-called *ala* or *cohors quingenaria* was commanded by a *praefectus* of equestrian rank.

There were a minority of larger-sized units, nominally *alae* or *cohortes milliariae*; these had 24 squadrons, or 10 centuries, commanded by a *tribunus*. The composition of a *cohors equitata milliaria* is uncertain: some scholars interpret it as having 10 centuries and 8 squadrons (i.e. 1,056 men), others only 4 cavalry squadrons (about 930 men in total).

Cohors II Afrorum Flavia	Numidia/Mauretania	AD 197–198
Cohors II Alpinorum equitata quingenaria	Ala Ubiorum, Germania Inf.	
	Pannonia	1st–2nd century AD
	Mursa, Dalmatia	2nd half 1st century AD
	Pannonia Inferior	AD 110
	Pannonia Superior	2nd half 2nd century AD
Cohors II Aquitanorum quingenaria equitata	Germania Superior & Raetia	2nd century AD
Cohors II Asturum equitata	Germania Inferior	1st century AD
	Britannia	2nd–3rd century AD
Cohors II Asturum et Callaecorum	Pannonia Inferior	2nd century AD
Cohors II Batavorum Victrix quingenaria, later milliaria	Germania Inferior	Claudius
	Britannia	AD 43–69
	Germania	AD 69–71
	Cannabiaca, Pannonia	2nd century AD
Cohors II Biturigium	Mogontiacum, Germania Inf.	AD 43
Cohors II Breucorum	Mauretania Caesariensis	AD 107
Cohors II Brittonum	Mauretania Caesariensis	AD 107
Cohors II Brittonum (Brittanorum) mill. CR PF	Vetera, Germania Inferior	AD 98
Cohors II Brittonum milliaria Nervia Pacensis	Pannonia Inferior	AD 114–145/160
Cohors II Cyrenaica Augusta equitata	Butzbach, Germania Superior	1st–2nd century AD
Cohors II Cyrrhestarum	Dalmatia	AD 6–9
	Germania Inferior	AD 70
Cohors II Dacorum Aurelia	Pannonia Inferior	AD 175–200
Cohors II Delmatorum eq.	Britannia	1st–3rd century AD
Cohors II Delmatorum mill.	Dalmatia	2nd century AD
Cohors II Gallorum	Mauretania Caesariensis	AD 107
Cohors II Gallorum equitata	Britannia	2nd–3rd century AD
Cohors II Hispana CR	Mauretania Tingitana	2nd century AD
Cohors II Hispanorum	Sedunum (Sion), Raetia	AD 50–100
Cohors II Hispanorum Vasconum equitata CR	Britannia & Mauretania Tingitana	2nd century AD
Cohors II Hispanorum peditata PF	Utrecht, Germania Inferior	Trajan
	Bologa, Pannonia	AD 110–115
Cohors II Lingonum equitata	Olicana (Ilkley) & Gabrosentum (Moresby), Britannia	mid-2nd century AD
Cohors II Maurorum mill.	Matrica, Pannonia Inferior	2nd half 2nd century AD
Cohors II Nerviorum CR	Hadrian's Wall, Britannia	2nd century AD
	Pannonia Inferior	AD 148
Cohors II Pannoniorum	Britannia	2nd century AD
Cohors II Raetorum	Germania	AD 82
	Raetia	2nd century AD
Cohors II Sardorum	Rapidum, M. Caesariensis	AD 122
Cohors II Syrorum Sagittariorum milliaria	Mauretania Tingitana	2nd century AD
Cohors II Thracum	Mannaricium (Buren Markt), Germania Inferior	1st century AD
	Britannia	AD 122
Cohors II Thracum equitata	Mumrills, Britannia	mid-2nd century AD
Cohors II Tungrorum mill.	Blatobulgium (Birrens), Britannia	mid-2nd century AD
Cohors II Varcianorum CR	Gelduba (Krefeld), Remagen, & Ara Ubiorum, Germ. Inf.	mid-2nd century AD
Cohors II Vasconorum	–	–
Cohors III Aquitanorum equitata CR	Stockstadt, Neckarburken & Osterburken, Germania Sup.	AD 74–160
Cohors III Asturum CR	Mauretania Tingitana	1st–2nd century AD
Cohors III Bracaugustanorum	Britannia	2nd century AD
Cohors III Breucorum	Wörden, Germania Inferior	1st–2nd century AD
Cohors III Brittanorum	Raetia	2nd century AD
Cohors III Delmatorum eq.	Germania	1st–2nd century AD
Cohors III Gallorum Felix equitata	Germania	AD 74
Cohors III Gallorum	Mauretania	2nd century AD
	Italica, Hispania Baetica	2nd half 2nd century AD
Cohors III Lingonum eq.	Britannia	2nd century AD
Cohors III Lusitanorum	Novaesium & Ara Ubiorum, Germania Inferior	2nd century AD
Cohors III Nerviorum CR	Britannia	2nd century AD
	Italica, Hispania Baetica	2nd half 2nd century AD
Cohors III Thracum CR	Künzing & Gnotzheim, Raetia	2nd century AD
Cohors IIII Aquitanorum quingenaria equitata CR	Germania	1st–2nd century AD
Cohors IIII Breucorum	Ara Ubiorum, Germania Inf.	1st century AD
	Britannia	2nd–3rd century AD
Cohors IIII Gallorum eq.	Camboglanna (Castlesteads), Britannia	Hadrian
	Raetia	AD 107 & 166
	Mauretania Tingitana	1st–2nd century AD
Cohors IIII Delmatorum	Bingium (Bingerbruck), Germania Superior	1st century AD
	Britannia	1st–2nd century AD
Cohors IIII Lingonum eq.	Britannia	2nd century AD
Cohors IIII Nerviorum	Britannia	AD 135
Cohors IIII Sugambrorum quingenaria	Mauretania Caesariensis	AD 107
Cohors IIII Tungrorum mill.	Noricum	AD 94
	Raetia	AD 129, 139 & 140
	Mauretania Tingitana	AD 153, 157 & 161
Cohors IIII Thracum PF	Valkenburg, Germania Inf.	Trajan
Cohors IIII Vindelicorum	Ara Ubiorum, Germania Inf.	1st century AD
	Grosskrotzenburg, Nida (Heddernheim),	

Unit	Location	Date
	Confluentes (Niederberg), Obenburg am Main, Germania Superior	1st–2nd century AD
ohors IIII Voluntariorum	Quadrata, Pannonia	2nd century AD
ohors V Asturum	Bonna, Germania Inferior	1st century AD
ohors V Baetica	Ilipula Minor (Los Corrales), Hispania Baetica	from c.AD 175
ohors V Breucorum	Noricum	1st–2nd century AD
ohors V Callaecorum Lucensium	Pannonia	2nd century AD
ohors V Delmatorum milliaria equitata CR	Germania	1st–2nd century AD
	Mauretania Tingitana	1st–2nd century AD
ohors V Gallorum	Transdierna (Tekija), Pannonia	1st–2nd century AD
	Britannia	AD 122
ohors V Hispanorum	Germania	AD 74
ohors V Nerviorum	Britannia	Hadrian
ohors V Raetorum quin.	Britannia	Hadrian
ohors VI Asturum	–	–
ohors VI Breucorum	Germania Inferior	1st–2nd century AD
ohors VI Delmatorum eq.	Mauretania Caesariensis	2nd century AD
ohors VI Gallorum	Hispania Tarraconensis	AD 150
ohors VI Ingenuorum	Vetera, Ara Ubiorum, & Colonia Ulpia Traiana, Germania Inferior	AD 151
ohors VI Nerviorum CR	Rough Castle, Aesica (Great Chesters), Magnis (Carvoran), Britannia	Antoninus Pius
ohors VI Raetorum	Germania Superior	AD 94
	Aesica, Britannia	2nd half 2nd century AD
ohors VI Thracum (eq.?)	Glevum, Britannia	1st century AD
ohors VI Voluntariorum	Dalmatia	AD 6–9
	Pannonia	AD 15–19
ohors VII Breucorum CR	Mogontiacum, Germania Inf.	AD 83–84
	Pannonia Inferior	AD 86–192
ohors VII Delmatorum eq.	Mauretania Caesariensis	AD 149–150
ohors VII Lusitanorum	–	–
ohors VII Raetorum	Germania	AD 74–82
ohors VII Thracum	Britannia	2nd century AD
ohors VIII Raetorum CR	Pannonia	Domitian
ohors VIII Voluntariorum CR	Dalmatia	AD 6–9
	Germania	AD 9–70
	Dalmatia	1st–2nd century AD
ohors XIII Urbana	Carthage, Africa Proconsularis	–
ohors XIII Urbana	Lugdunum, G. Lugdunensis	2nd century AD
ohors XIV Urbaniciana	Lugdunum	1st century AD
ohors XV Voluntariorum CR	Wörden or Ara Ubiorum, Germania Inferior	2nd century AD
ohors XVI Urbaniciana	Lugdunum	1st century AD
ohors XVIII Urbaniciana	Lugdunum	AD 69
ohors XVIII Voluntariorum	Gerulata, Pannonia Superior	2nd century AD
	Kosmaj, Dalmatia	2nd half 2nd century AD
ohors XXX Voluntariorum	Germania Superior	Antoninus Pius
ohors XXXII Voluntariorum CR	Sisak, Pannonia	1st–2nd century AD
	Germania Superior	Flavian period
ra Ubiorum Colonia Agrippina	Cologne, Germania Inferior	
r Ara Colonia Ulpia Traiana	Xanten, Germania Inferior	from AD 151

Alae:

Unit	Location	Date
la (Gallorum) Agrippiana miniata	Germania Superior	pre-Claudian
	Britannia	2nd century AD
la Asturum	Cavillonum (Chalon-sur-Saône), Gallia Lugdunensis	2nd–3rd century AD
la Augusta (Gallorum) Proculeiana	Cilurnum (Chesters), Britannia	2nd century AD
la Augusta Gallorum Petriana milliaria CR	Coria/Corstopitum (Corbridge), Britannia	AD 84–105
la Augusta Vocontiorum	Germania Inferior	1st century AD
	Trimontium (Newstead), Britannia	c.AD 120
la Equitum (?)	Mursa, Dalmatia	end 1st century AD
la (Gallorum) Piacentia	Germania Superior	pre-AD 82
	Britannia	2nd century AD
la (Hispanorum) Vettonum CR	Britannia	1st–3rd century AD
la Noricorum	Germania Inferior	AD 77–167
	Pannonia	AD 81–96
la Parthorum	Pisoraca, H.Tarraconensis	28 BC–AD 70
la (Gallorum) Sebosiana	Britannia	2nd–3rd century AD
la I (Hispanorum) Aravacorum	Mauretania Caesariensis	mid-2nd century AD
	Brigetio, Pannonia	2nd half 2nd century AD
la I Asturum	Condercum (Benwell), Britannia	2nd–3rd century AD
la I Britannica	Brigetio, Pannonia	AD 150
	Mauretania Caesariensis	2nd half 2nd century AD
la I Caninafatium	Pannonia & M. Caesariensis	mid-2nd century AD
la I Contariorum	Pannonia & M. Caesariensis	mid-2nd century AD
la I Ituraeorum	Pannonia	AD 148
	Mauretania Caesariensis	AD 149–150
la I (Pannoniorum) Sebosiana	Britannia	2nd–3rd century AD
la I (Pannoniorum) Tampiana	Britannia, then Noricum	2nd century AD
la I Thracum	Britannia	1st–2nd century AD
	Germania Inferior	2nd century AD
la I Tungrorum	Britannia	1st–2nd century AD
la II Aravacorum	Dalj, Pannonia	AD 85
	Mursa, Pannonia	end 1st century AD?
la II Asturum	Cilurnum, Britannia	2nd–3rd century AD
la II Flavia Hispanorum CR	Petavonium, Hispania Tarraconensis	from AD 96
la II Pannoniorum	Solina, Dalmatia	2nd century AD
	Szombathely, Dura, Stari Slankamen & Belegisa, Pannonia	2nd–3rd century AD

Fragment of sculpture representing a Gallo-Roman cavalryman in the army of the Principate, 1st century AD, from Mediolanum (Saintes) in Aquitania. This exceptional sculpture is reconstructed as Plate A3; it reveals the simultaneous use of a Roman *lorica squamata* and a Celtic torque at the neck. (Musée Archéologique de Saintes, inv. num. 1949.457A; photo courtesy the Museum)

ARMS & EQUIPMENT

Modern scholars suppose that, during the early Empire, mass-produce equipment was made available to legionaries and auxiliaries. While this true within certain limits, we must avoid imagining a schematized 'class panoply' of equipment for either legionary or auxiliary. The notion of 'uniform' did not exist at that time, and differences of equipment were the rule even within the same unit. Certain supplies of similar weapons, armou and other gear were issued, but men were free to purchase more or le decorated versions according to their tastes and their pockets. Moreove as underlined by the works of Oldenstein and Bishop, some finds from military campsites show characteristic signs of being scrap intended fc recycling by *fabricae* (workshops) in the repair, adaptation or production of items for locally based units – for instance, at Corbridge and Newstead i northern Britain. The Roman soldier was responsible for the upkeep of h weapons, and a part of his salary was deducted to pay for this. When he wa discharged his unit would buy the weapons back from him, so he woul recover that money.

As suggested by Bishop, the distribution of archaeological material i the provinces may indicate the types of troops present there, but shoul be interpreted with caution. For example, finds of horse harness do no necessarily mean that a cavalry unit was present, since horses were als found in infantry camps. The present author believes that the attributio of certain equipment finds specifically to a legionary or auxilia infantryman or a cavalry trooper is, at best, speculative unless supporte by iconographic and written sources. Such sources, when available, ca help in interpreting the appearance of the soldiers stationed in a particula territory.

Of course, Tacitus clearly states (*Hist.*, I, 38) that the arms provided b the state to legionaries and auxiliaries showed basic differences. During th civil war of AD 69 the Emperor Otho ordered 'the armoury to be opened The soldiers immediately seized the arms without regard to rule or militar order, no distinction being observed between Praetorians and legionarie both of whom indiscriminately took the shields *(scuta)* and helmets *(galea* of the auxiliary troops...'. However, if equipment defined by moder scholars as 'legionary' is excavated in the context of an auxiliary camp o fort, the most straightforward explanation is that it was indeed used b *auxilia* – and this interpretation is sometimes supported by the iconograph The purpose of this book is to describe representative evidence for th variety and complexity of Roman military equipment in the differen provinces, and even within the same units.

THE PROVINCES:

GALLIA AQUITANIA

A relief from Mediolanum (Saintes) shows either local auxiliary troops o legionaries from the nearby camp at Aunedonnacum (Aulnay-de-Saintonge wearing the laminated armour called (in the modern term) *lorica segmentat* (see page 5). Today there is a growing body of opinion that this armou was not worn exclusively by legionary troops (as suggested by earlie interpretations of Trajan's Column), and this revisionist view is based no only upon archaeological evidence from a number of auxiliary forts of th

Tiberian-Flavian period, but also on iconographic evidence. In fact, Trajan's Column itself does not show exclusively legionaries wearing segmented armour and auxiliaries clad in ringmail. In scenes XLVI–XLVIII soldiers attacking the Dacians wear mail and leather, but carry legionary *pila* javelins and oval shields marked with an eagle – a clear legionary symbol.

Finds at Aulnay-de-Saintonge dated to AD 21–43 include characteristic bronze buckles and clasps from laminated armour, perhaps belonging to soldiers of Legio XIV Gemina or Legio II Augusta. Leaf-shaped javelin heads found in the camp are similar to those on the relief from Mediolanum. Horse-harness pendants here attest the presence of cavalry, as confirmed by the Mediolanum sculptures. Numerous squared plates from the *cingulum* military belt typical of the period, decorated with niello, have been found. The site also yielded *dona militaria* (military decorations) such as a silver *armilla*; *fibulae* brooches for military cloaks; tools such as the sheath of a *dolabra* (camping pickaxe); and blacksmith's tongs. A workshop was located in the south-west part of the camp, and this explains why many finds, such as embossed *umbones* for rectangular shields, had a particularly Celtic appearance.

Grave finds at Neuvy-Pailloux, near Argentomagus (Indre), include important cavalry helmet masks dated to AD 40–50. It is known that organized auxiliary units within the Roman army continued to fight with their national weapons during at least the 1st century AD. In the tombs of Gallo-Roman aristocrats *torques*, and swords of Celtic types, were found alongside Roman belts and mail armour; a grave at Dun-sur-Auron (50–20 BC) yielded three Celtic-made swords, three spearheads and the fragments of a dagger.

GALLIA BELGICA

Considerable amounts of equipment have been recovered from the river Saône. Ringmail, in one case of bronze (probably forming the edges of an iron armour), was recovered near Pons Dubis (Pontoux), and part of an armour combining ringmail and ridged scales *(plumata)* was found near Mendeure.

A relief at Arlon shows Roman cavalrymen with a helmet used from the reign of Augustus, the 'Weiler' type so-called from the location of the first specimen found in 1981. This type has an iron skull or bowl bearing a thin applied layer of silver or bronze repoussé, often embossed in imitation of human hair. A frontal brow band is drawn up in a central point like a diadem; the neck-guard is narrow, but the cheek-pieces are wide and include realistic embossed ears. Evolved examples often have the 'diadem' embossed with images of *dona militaria*. We may detect a particular taste for decoration which was probably characteristic of the cavalry, especially in the 1st century AD; but, since the same type is visible in the aforementioned relief from Mediolanum, this helmet was also in use by some infantry.

What Robinson calls the 'Imperial Gallic' helmet (Weisenau type) of the Roman legionary, used in all the provinces, was an evolution from the

Detail from a relief of cavalrymen on a pillar tomb from Arlon in Belgica, third quarter of 1st century AD. Note the unmistakable depiction of the shoulder plates from a *lorica segmentata* worn in conjunction with mail or leather armour; see reconstruction as Plate A4. Note that one helmet has the embossed 'hair' effect, and both show the pronounced 'ears' associated with the Weiler typology. (Drawing by Andrea Salimbeti, ex-Miks-Davoli)

Celtic Agen-Port typology already used by the legions in the mid-1s century BC. A splendid specimen from Vesontio (Besançon), dated to A∎ 25–50, is ornamented with a copper-alloy band around the brow and wit∎ insertions of red enamel. (In this text the terms copper-alloy, brass an∎ bronze are used simply to describe hardened yellow metal.) Classified b∎ Robinson as Imperial Gallic Type F, it is made of iron between 1mm an∎ 1.5mm thick, and may originally have been silvered. Decorativ∎ copper-alloy rivets are clearly visible on the cheek-guards, and copper-allo∎ holders for feather plumes are riveted to each side above these. Th∎ interior shows traces of leather from the lining which must have bee∎ present in all Roman helmets. The brow has the grooved 'eyebrows∎ typical of this category of helmets, above a strong riveted-on defensive ba∎ protecting the skull from frontal impacts.

A specimen of the long-pointed category of *gladius Hispaniensis* sword∎ termed the Mainz type after the first find, comes from Mâcon, and example∎ of the shorter-pointed Pompeii type from Mailly le Porte and Simandre∎ The former type was characteristic of the Augustan-Claudian period, an∎ the latter of the second half of the 1st century AD, but both were in us∎ until the end of the 2nd century. Analysis of Mainz-type scabbard fragment∎ from Thorey, Saint-Marcel and Mâcon has revealed that they were made ∎ alder and linden wood, and bronze fittings at the mouth survive on th∎ Mâcon scabbard.

The *pugio* (military dagger) belonged to the same panoply as the *gladiu∎* and a dagger scabbard preserved in the Musée Denon has a clasp ver∎ similar to those fitted to *gladii* scabbards. The scabbard of the Allério∎ dagger, splendidly preserved with its characteristic decorations in ename∎ and silver, belongs to a common typology found among camps north of th∎ Alps dated precisely to the reign of Claudius. The characteristic *pilu∎* (javelin) has also been discovered in the Saône; one with a rectangula∎ socket, from Thorey, is a fine example of the late Caesarian or earl∎ Augustan period.

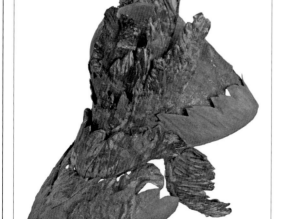

Right side of senior officer's helmet of gilded bronze, 1st century AD, from Gallia Lugdunensis. It is basically of Etrusco-Corinthian shape, but the area normally occupied by the face-guard is exaggeratedly large, and embossed with eyebrows, eyes and nose (not visible from this angle). The lower rim is reinforced with an applied band of embossed acanthus leaves, and a large laurel wreath is attached at the back and projects forward at each side of the skull. (Musée Rolin, Autun; photo courtesy Andrei Negin)

GALLIA LUGDUNENSIS

Lugdunum (Lyon), seat of an important garrison, ha∎ revealed examples of ringmail. Mail was widely used i∎ Gaul, as revealed by the fragments found in the grave∎ of elite cavalrymen such as that at Chassenard. This wa∎ probably the grave of a Gallo-Roman cavalry officer, ∎ chieftain of the Aedui serving under the emperor∎ Tiberius or Caligula. His mail shirt was still fitted wit∎ the archaic bronze double hook on the breast to secur∎ the *humeralia* (shoulder-doublings). The Chassenar∎ grave also yielded the best specimen of a mask helme∎ found in this province, designed not only for th∎ Hippika Gymnasia cavalry sports but also for battle. I∎ the same grave were an iron sword (originally wit∎ scabbard), a bronze *torques*, a leaf-shaped spearhead, a∎ iron arrowhead, and four plates and the buckle from ∎ splendid silver-plated belt.

Squamae (scales) from scale armours have bee∎ found widely at Lyon and in other locations in Gaul∎ and laminated armour was said to have been adapte∎

om the segmented armours of the Crupellarii of the *schola* of
ugustodunum (Autun). One of the most discussed Roman officer helmets
omes from Lugdunum: the specimen dated to the Flavian era, decorated
ith an applied laurel crown, which is now preserved in the Musée Rolin
t Autun. According to some authors this massive piece, of Etrusco-
Corinthian typology, was made to be added to a statue, but its dimensions
t the human head well. Etrusco-Corinthian helmets are still visible on
nany monuments representing gods and generals of the early Empire, and
ere the prototypes for some 3rd-century helmet specimens, so there is no
eason to suppose that the Lugdunum helmet was not made for wear;
obinson proposed that it might have belonged to some legate or provincial
overnor.

The bronze craftsmen of Alesia, whose expertise in tinning metals was
ecorded by Pliny the Elder, produced harness fittings for Roman troops
1 the province and for the legions on the Rhine *limes*.

GALLIA NARBONENSIS

rom the Caesarian and early Imperial periods the great reliefs of Narbonne
Narbo Martius), station of Julius Caesar's famous Legio X, illustrate the
quipment of Roman legionaries in the province. 'Muscled' armours in
eather or bronze are clearly represented, worn over *subarmales* (arming
erkins) having various arrangements of *pteryges* (hanging edge-straps). The
hields show details of *deigmata* (blazons), and are mainly of the semi-
ylindrical polygonal or oval types, but include the round bronze *clipea* of
fficers. The *gladii* are mainly of Mainz type, and a variety of *hastae, pilae*
nd other spears and javelins are represented, among helmets of Hellenic,
mperial Gallic and Coolus typologies.

Shirts of mail are also depicted, so it is not surprising to see the marching
Augustan legionaries on the relief from Glanum clad in mail shirts, with
mperial Gallic Type A helmets and quadrangular shields. The relief from
relatum (Arles), dated to about the time of Sacrovir's revolt in AD 21,
hows soldiers and officers of the Gallic legions clad in muscle, scale, and
Hellenic corselets fitted with *pteryges* and worn over heavy padded tunics.
Coolus and Buggenum-Montefortino helmets are among the types
epresented, ornamented with tall plumes; *gladii* are shown worn on either
ide of the body. A *signum*-bearer
lad in muscle armour and wearing
lionskin over his head carries a
ound shield under his left arm.

Also from the Tiberian period, a
ariety of equipment is represented
n the Arch of Orange (Arausius).
centurion clad in ringmail wears,
ke some of the legionaries, the
ew type of Imperial Gallic helmet
f Weisenau typology (see above),
esides helmets of Haguenau,
Buggenum or Coolus type. The
egionaries have rectangular semi-
ylindrical shields, the cavalrymen
val or rhomboid shields complete
vith an *umbo* following the local

Statue of an Augustan-period
Gallo-Roman officer from
Vachères, Basses-Alpes, wearing
a coat of mail with characteristic
humeralia (shoulder-doublings);
see reconstruction as Plate A1.
(Musée Calvet, Avignon, cast in
Museo della Civiltà Romana;
author's photos)

Detail from the 1st-century AD
stele of Rufus Sita, a trooper of
Cohors VI Thracum, from Glevum
(Gloucester); note the brow band
rising to a central point like a
diadem. The contemporary stele
of Dolanus of *Cohors IIII
Thracum*, from Aquae
Mattiacorum in Germania
Superior and now in Wiesbaden
Museum, shows a very similar
helmet, but with the 'diadem'
heavily decorated. The bowl of a
similar Attic iron helmet has
been recovered at Trimontium
(Newstead, Scotland), although it
now lacks any fittings.
(Gloucester Museum; drawing by
Andrei Negin)

Horse-harness *phalera* from Deva (Chester), the legionary fortress of *Legio XX Valeria Victrix* in the 2nd century AD. This particular example of one of the most common decorative objects seen on Roman military gear shows a strong Celtic influence – a (severed?) human head with long hair. It reminds us that local production would introduce variations among the accoutrements made in the different provinces. (Deva Museum; author's photo, courtesy the Museum)

Reproduction of the 2nd or 3rd-century AD stele of Caecilius Avitus from Deva. The inscription translates as: 'To the spirits of the departed: Caecilius Avitus, from Emerita Augusta [Mérida, capital of Lusitania], Optio of Legio XX Valeria Victrix, served for 15 years, died at the age of 34; his heir had this made'. He carries the staff of his rank, and writing tablets in his left hand. There is plentiful evidence that the clothing, hair, etc. of figures carved on stelae were originally painted, and remaining traces of colour were noted by 19th-century scholars (see discussion in MAA 374, *Roman Military Clothing (1): 100 BC–AD 200*). This reproduction has been finished with a brown *paenula* cloak and staff and a blue tunic. (Grosvenor Museum, Chester; author's photo, courtesy the Museum)

models. The devices on the shields (e.g. the wings of Jupiter's eagle, the Capricorn) indicate the blazons of Legio II Augusta. The site of Vasio (Vaison la Romaine) has yielded one of the few fragments of the *lorica segmentata* found in the Gallic provinces.

BRITANNIA

The Hod Hill excavations yielded important finds from the Claudian invasion army: *pila* of the type found in Germania Inferior, *squamae*, and helmets. Archaeologists were aided by the recovery of spearheads from the Roman *hasta* in a precise chronological context. Lincoln also offers examples of the same leaf-shaped spearheads, with narrow elongated specimens having a slightly pronounced rib; all belong to the earlier phase of the invasion, and are similar to spears found in Germania Superior. In Corbridge on the northern frontier leaf-shaped spearheads of rhomboidal section have been found. Spear and javelin heads from Newstead, Scotland, dated to the late 1st and early 2nd century, are mainly leaf-shaped, and vary from 25cm to 35cm (9.8–13.7in) long. Shaft fragments surviving in sockets from Newstead are of hazel wood.

The gravestone of a Hamian (Syrian) archer at Housesteads on Hadrian's Wall, from *c*.AD 125–150, confirms the use by these auxiliaries of a conical pointed helmet, perhaps similar to the framed *Spangenhelm* worn by Eastern *simmachiarii* represented on Trajan's Column, or to a globular pointed helmet in Zagreb Archaeological Museum. This stele also shows the characteristic appearance of the Levantine bowmen, with the Roman *cingulum* military belt, and *feminalia* breeches worn beneath the tunic. Fragments of a bow from the mid-2nd-century Antonine fort at Bar Hill show composite construction.

The *lorica segmentata* hoard discovered at Corbridge in 1964 was a revolutionary find, which allowed Charles Daniels and H. Russell Robinson to attempt the reconstruction of the most famous of Roman armour types. The well-preserved contents of the hoard also included tools, weaponry, wax writing tablets and papyrus. Dating from between AD 122 and 138, the armour were in excellent condition due to their having been buried in an iron-bound, leather-covered wooden chest, and may be attributed to an infantry cohort. By contrast, evidence for a later stage in the evolution of the *lorica segmentata* comes from a cavalry fort at Newstead (Trimontium), where it was found together with a variety of equipment including ornate cavalry 'sports' helmets and horse fittings including ronze saddle plates and studded leather chamfrons. The author believes that it is therefore probable that in the case of Trimontium this armour would have been issued to cavalry troopers.

The large number of fittings from laminated armours found at British tes indicates that the hinges and clasps of this type of cuirass were specially prone to breakage, and that armours were often repaired in ifferent ways in local workshops. This might explain the differences etween the types of fastenings visible on the Columns of Trajan and arcus Aurelius.

Corselets of leather or linen and ringmail armour are visible on mbstones. The present author believes that the armour of the Claudian-eriod centurion Favonius Facilis from Colchester is an example of the rmer type, made of organic material. Given the bad state of preservation f his tombstone, it is unclear if the Hamian archer at Housesteads is quipped with mail armour or with a leather corselet like that worn by his ossible countrymen on Trajan's Column. The mail shirt used by infantry r cavalry was usually short-sleeved and fell to the hips, with the edges either raight or 'dagged' in points. Various fragments of mail have been found British sites such as Newstead, the Lunt Fort (Baginton), and Carlingwark och in Kirkcudbrightshire. The particularly rich specimens from Newstead re made of punched and riveted rings, while the fragment from the Lunt ort is of fine bronze.

A shield from Doncaster, with bronze fittings, represents one of the ost interesting finds related to the auxiliary units in Britannia. It is ctangular in shape, slightly convex, and made of three layers of wood lued together. Its applied metal plates and rivets are particularly notable, s is its hemispherical boss, which protects a large vertical reinforcement n the inside serving as a handgrip. Once again, it contradicts the ontention by some scholars that the auxiliaries carried only oval-shaped nields.

Horse-harness fittings from Newstead include three-piece af-shaped pendants; these emerged during the Tiberian-laudian period, and went out of style following the Flavian eriod. Some examples are silver-plated and decorated with ylized foliate motifs.

At Longthorpe, Cambridgeshire, occupied by Legio IX lispana and an auxiliary cavalry force in AD 61–62 at the test, large quantities of cavalry as well as legionary equipment ere found.

ERMANIA INFERIOR

ome legionaries represented on stelae in the Germanic rovinces are equipped with shafted weapons, and especially ne *pilum* – for example, that of Quintus Petilius from the gionary fortress at Bonn. Characteristic of the first two enturies of the Principate, this javelin had a pyramidal or arbed head ideal for piercing shields and armours, at the end f a long, thin iron shank attached to a wooden shaft. By the me of Augustus the tang inserted into the shaft was usually erforated with two or three rivet holes, and the junction was einforced with a metal collar shaped like a truncated pyramid, tting over the top of the shaft and secured by four small iron

Stele of the cavalryman Romanius of *Ala Noricorum*, 1st century AD, from Mainz. The Weiler-type helmet is clearly depicted, and note the length of the *spatha* sword. Just visible in the background at the left of the photo is the trooper's servant carrying two javelins. (Römisch-Germanisches Zentralmuseum, Mainz; photo courtesy Dr Stefano Izzo)

wedges. Three specimens from Oberaden are preserved with intact head shanks, collars, and substantial portions of the wooden shaft. The iron part varies between 49cm and 70cm (19.3–27.5in) in length; the slim trapezoidal tang was secured by three rivets in the longer specimen, two rivets in the shorter ones. In all three the lower part of the iron shank is square in section, but rounded as it tapers towards the head. The *pilum* is relevant to the identification of legionary units from auxiliaries in monuments on which both appear: according to Tacitus, the legionary was armed with the *pilum* and auxiliaries with the simple *hasta* spear.

The stelae of Tiberian-period cavalrymen in Germania are among the earliest evidence for a new type of helmet for the cavalry, the so-called Weiler type (see above, 'Gallia Belgica'). Most of these tombstones clearly depict helmets with small neck-guards and diadem-like frontal bands, and some of them show skull decoration in the form of curly hair; we can also see wide, decorated cheek-pieces covering the ears (e.g., that of Flavius Bassus of the Ala Noricorum from Cologne). Two splendid specimens of this type of iron helmet were recovered at Castra Vetera (Xanten). One has carefully interlaced geometric motifs representing hair; it seems that this example had only the edges of the ears and the frontal diadem covered with sheet silver. The second has tinned brass hair incorporating a brass laurel crown in relief; the frontal diadem is ornamented with small boss representing an emperor (either Caligula or Claudius).

Striking examples of face-mask helmets have also been discovered. An iron mask from Kops Plateau, Nijmegen, found by accident in 1983, was part of a two-piece helmet; pierced for the eyes and mouth, the mask did not possess the ears seen on others of the same type. A hinge at the centre of the forehead originally joined it to the brow of the helmet.

Copper-alloy embossed scabbard chape for a *gladius* of Mainz typology from Vindonissa, dated to AD 16–46. It measures 137mm x 60mm (5.3 x 2.3in), and the upper part shows the ever-popular motif of a Roman cavalryman triumphing over a barbarian warrior. (Author's photo, courtesy Brugg Museum)

The equipment of legionaries and auxiliaries in the province is visible on gravestones of the 1st and 2nd centuries, and the battle equipment of one resident legion, Legio Minervia, can be identified on Trajan's Column. The rare standard borne by one *signifer* can only be that of this legion, so the legionaries drawn up around him must show the blazon of that legion on their rectangular shields. They are well represented, imposingly clad in the iron *lorica segmentata* whose fastening system and shoulder plates appear similar to the Newstead and Carnuntum models. Their helmets are of Imperial Italic typology, many of them covered by the crossed protective bars of the period and surmounted by a ring; their swords, of Pompeii type, are suspended on the right side of the body from a *cingulum bullatum* (bossed baldric). The *signifer* wears ringmail over a *subarmalis* and a second inner garment, perhaps the *thorax laneus* mentioned by Suetonius. The *cornicen* trumpeter is wearing similar equipment, and both he and the standard-bearer have their heads covered by wild animal skins.

However, the stele of Quintus Petilius of Legio XV Primigenia from Bonn shows that oval shields were also in use by legionaries in Germania Inferior, as further confirmed by excavations at the legionary camp of Valkenburg (Praetorium Agrippinae) where leather covers for oval shields have been found.

(Continued on page 3)

A

1

4

2

3

B

1

2

4

3

F

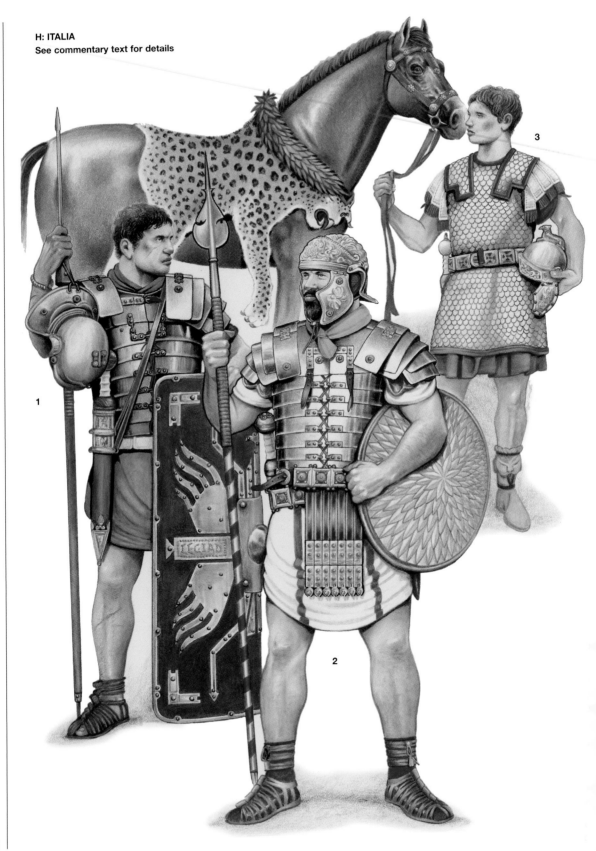

The employment of the *pilum* is again strongly attested by the archaeology and iconography, e.g. on the gravestone of Caius Crispus from Wiesbaden. Iron fragments including a collar fitting have been found on the site of the battle of the Teutoburg Forest near Kalkriese. Other kinds of javelins were also used, especially in the 1st and 2nd centuries AD by *auxilia*, who could carry two or three light throwing spears simultaneously; evidence comes from the stelae of Annaius Daverzus of Cohors IIII Delmatorum from Bingerbrück-Bingium, and of Licaius of Cohors I Pannonium from Wiesbaden. Several light javelins might be carried by cavalrymen in a quiver or by their *calones* (servants), as seen on the stele of Romanius of Ala Noricorum. Javelin heads, often found on German sites, might be pyramidal or leaf-shaped. From Haltern, Mainz, Augst, Rheingönheim and Vindonissa archaeologists recovered specimens of leaf-shaped spearheads and spear butts/ferrules of the 1st century AD. Among the weapons used by the Rhine legionaries was the *hasta amentata*, i.e. a spear fitted with a throwing thong (Is., *Et.* XVIII, 6), as carried by the legionary Flavoleius Cordus (Mainz Museum).

Arrowheads have been found in huge numbers; examples of the fifth group classified by Radman-Livaja (socketed flat-bladed heads) came from Vindonissa, dated between AD 13 and 100. In Mainz even older examples of this type have been excavated, dating from the end of the 1st century BC, and specimens from Aliso (Haltern) are contemporary with the first occupation of Germania between 11 BC and AD 16. However, lengths and weights of such finds vary widely, between 6cm and 12cm (2.3–4.7in) and 25–75g (0.88–2.64oz), so examples from Vindonissa have been categorized as arrowheads, and those from Aliso as catapult bolts or light javelins.

Weiler-type helmets are represented on the tombstones of 1st-century cavalrymen, e.g. that of Romanius from Mainz. Buckle fragments from laminated armour come from Hofheim, Vindonissa, Mainz and Dangestetten. The latter should belong to Legio XIX, destroyed under Varus, and, like some examples from Vindonissa, are identical to one found on the large shoulder-guard of an armour of Kalkriese typology found on that battlefield.

The rectangular *scutum* (shield) was not in fact peculiar to the legions: infantry units bearing the name '*scutata*' would have had them, as shown on Trajan's Column. Some stelae show legionaries with the oval *scuta* (e.g. Licaius), and *auxilia* (e.g. Annaius Daverzus) with rectangular examples. This latter was fitted with a central hemispherical *umbo* embossed out of a rectangular plate (e.g. a fine specimen from Vindonissa), but in the archaeology these plates are much less common than simple circular ones associated with oval shields. The shield of the legionary might have been either the classical oval shape (see Plate F1 for our reconstruction of Caius Castricius Victor of Legio II Adiutrix serving in Pannonia); a semi-cylindrical rectangle; or a variation of that with rounded-off corners, as indicated by the leather shield-covers found at Vindonissa.

The province has yielded pieces of appliqué metal shield fittings, as nailed to the wood through the fabric covering of the surface. From Mainz came fragments of iron *fulgures* (lightning-bolts) of the 1st century AD, and from Emlichheim a bronze Capricorn. These finds raise the question of whether the *fulgures* were generally applied in metal or only painted. The sources and the archaeology argue in favour of iconographic

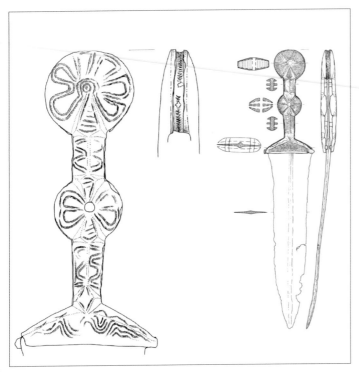

Roman *pugio* (military dagger) found near Štanjel – today in the Karst region of Western Slovenia – and dating from the 1st century BC/1st century AD. The hilt is of 'sandwich' construction, with two external iron plates encasing wooden parts on both sides of a flat tang forged in one piece with the blade; the tang follows the shape of the hilt including the round expansion in the middle. The wood is partly preserved only in the pommel, where the end of the tang was pushed into it. The overall length is 29.5cm (11.6in); the blade is 18.7cm (7.2in) long, with a pronounced midrib, but lacks the more markedly waisted shape often seen. (National Museum of Slovenia, no. Zn 112; drawings by Andrea Salimbeti, ex-Istenič)

evidence which shows the lightning-bolts on the shields in raised relief. An interesting reference comes from the 1st-century poet Valerius Flaccus, who writes in his *Argonautica* (VI, 54, 6): 'All the phalanx wear embossed on the shield the device of Jupiter, and the spread fires of the trident-shaped lightning bolts [*trifida fulgures*], and you, Roman soldiers, are not the first to wear on your shields the rays and the shining wings of the flashing thunderbolt'. In another passage Flaccus (I, 496) describes shields shining in the sun, which suggests metallic appliqués. This is explicitly supported by a passage from Virgil (*Aen.*, VIII, 424, 30) which describes the working of weapons in Vulcan's forge; the *fulmines* (lights) on the shield were realized in iron because this metal was considered meteoric and thus of divine origin.

Vindonissa and other localities (Hofheim, Mainz, Wiesbaden) have provided various two-piece D-shaped bronze buckles with volutes and a triangular cross-section, used for fastening the soldier's belts; some are also silver-plated, and have a lily-shaped prong. Their form is typical of the 1st century, but they still appear on Trajan's Column. Finds from Vindonissa, Mainz and Aventicum (Avenches) include the best examples of 1st-century button-and-loop fasteners which served either as belt buckles or to fasten the dagger scabbard to the belt. Heart-shaped examples framed with perforation in the form of a *pelta* shield were positioned at the end of the belt, with a loop at the other end into which the button was fastened. Fittings from the Roman soldier's typical 'apron' have been found in great numbers; some of them are rectangular, either plain or decorated with engraving (Vindonissa, Aventicum).

A variety of horse-harness fittings found in this province include bronze mounts for bridle reins (Vindonissa, Hofheim, Aventicum). Leaf-shaped harness pendants – variously undecorated, with linear decoration, or of three-piece construction – were found at Mainz, Vindonissa, Hofheim, Aventicum, and the auxiliary camp at Ara Flaviae (Rottweil).

RAETIA

The leaf-shaped spearheads found in this province, especially in the *castella* on the Danube (Aislingen, Oberstimm and Ellingen-Sablonetum), have a useful chronological context; they date from the 1st and 2nd centuries AD, and those from Ellingen were probably issued to troops stationed there after AD 120.

An iron Imperial Gallic helmet was recovered from the Lech River at Augsburg. It retains the hinge bar of the left cheek-guard; on the right the remains of the bronze guard, apparently tin-plated, can be seen beneath the copper securing rivets. The presence of other, differently shaped holes ggests that the cheek-guards had been placed at some stage. The remains of ined copper rivets beneath the neck-guard re probably attachment points for the -laces. The helmet retains traces of silver eet beneath the surviving rivets for the ow band, on the top beneath the pper-alloy sheet where the crest holder s originally attached, and at the right-hand ge of the neck-guard. This suggests that ost of the helmet was silver-plated, set off contrasting elements in yellow metal.

Fragments of the *lorica segmentata* have en found at the Limes fort of Aalen. From raß-Moos on the Donau equipment for e cavalry Hippika Gymnasia is attested by, among other items, a splendid ce-mask of Hellenic typology. Horse-harness fittings similar to those found Germania Superior were discovered near Friedberg.

Military daggers in their scabbards decorated with brass and enamel; late 1st century BC/ early 1st century AD, from Siscia (modern Sisak), Pannonia. (Zagreb Archaeological Museum; photo courtesy Dr Ivan Radman-Livaja)

ORICUM

early iron dagger found in the late 1990s near the town of Štanjel, and nserved by the National Museum of Slovenia, is illustrated herewith. agdalensberg (ancient Virunum) has yielded rare specimens of *pila* with af-shaped heads. Belt plates from Noricum are unusual in showing mbossed hunting motifs, and the scene of the she-wolf suckling Romulus d Remus. Examples from Magdalensberg, which was abandoned in about D 45, confirm their use until the Claudian period, and they may be ntemporary with niello-inlaid specimens. Harness fittings from agdalensberg include numerous three-piece leaf-shaped pendants. Fine amples of *dolabrae* pickaxes come from the same locality; this military-issue ol was used to dig trenches, fell trees and work timber, but also as a apon.

ANNONIA & ILLYRICUM

x almost complete early Imperial *pila*, with pyramidal heads, have been covered near Sisak, and date from the Augustan conquest of Pannonia. me show the tang at the end of the shank perforated with only one rivet le (like a similar specimen from Vrhnica/Nauportus). Leaf-shaped earheads were found during the excavation of several Roman sites, and o from Sisak have recently been published by Radman-Livaja; one has a ghtly more pronounced lower part, comparable to specimens from Raetia, ermania Superior and Inferior. Another specimen from the same locality s a more rounded leaf-shaped blade tapering gradually towards the tip, e 1st-century examples from those provinces and Britannia; others, from rnuntum and Sisak, have the same shape as those from Hod Hill. nnonia also offers spearheads of elongated shape and rectangular section; amples from Sisak are variously dated between the 1st century BC and the rly 3rd century AD. The military *castrum* of Celemantia (modern Izsa) has vealed leaf-shaped spearheads 25–26cm (9.8–10.2in) long, javelin heads cluding pyramidal *pila*, an important specimen of a cavalry *contus* (lance), d various ferrules. The latter, of polygonal and hemispherical section, ve also been found at Ljubliana (Julia Aemona) and Sisak. These

Stele of the legionary Caius Castricius Victor of *Legio II Adiutrix* serving in Pannonia, c.AD 80–105. Note the helmet crest flanked by what have been interpreted as side feathers, but more closely resemble horns; the two javelins; the extensive 'apron' of straps over the groin and thighs; and the oval shield with a legionary blazon – see reconstruction as Plate F1. (Park of Aquincum Archaeological Museum, Budapest; author's photo, courtesy the Museum)

sharpened butt-caps allowed spears to be stuck into the groun either during a rest on the march or when preparing to receive charge; they could also be used offensively if the spearhead g broken off during combat.

The older style of military dagger is represented by tw magnificent specimens from Siscia (see photo, page 35), and recent find from Nauportus. Examples of the 2nd-century caval *spatha* sword, longer than the legionary *gladius*, come from Izs one, 88.5cm (34.8in) long, is analogous to finds from Sisa Carnuntum and also Newstead, and a second, 79cm (31in) lon recalls the Canterbury typology.

Lorica segmentata buckles from Sisak and Ljubliana attest th employment of this armour among local legionaries (and perha auxiliaries) – hardly surprising, given the extensive milita infrastructure of this province in early Imperial times. Fragmen of laminated cuirasses from Izsa are similar to those from Corbrid and Newstead.

Helmets of Weisenau (Imperial Gallic) typology are well attest in Pannonia, and even a centurion's helmet has been recovere from Sisak. However, cheek-guards found at Izsa echo Pannoni tombstones of the last quarter of the 2nd century in showing th employment by the legions of a new helmet, made of iron but wi extensive applied yellow-metal strips: the so-called Niederbieber typ Although classified by Robinson as Imperial Cavalry Type D, this gener shape would be used widely in the Roman army at least until the early 5 century. On the stele of the Severan-period *optio* Aelius Septimus of Leg II Adiutrix it is represented in the variant found at Osterburken, b showing all the characteristics of its typology. This kind of helmet had deep and almost vertical neck-guard; high cutouts around the ear reinforced with yellow-metal flanges; and cheek-guards over the ears an almost completely enclosing the face, with out-turned lower flanges protect the neck and fastened together by a metal pin under the chin.

This new model appears at the end of the 2nd century, in variants use by both cavalry and infantry; it gradually replaced the Imperial Gallic an Imperial Italic typologies, which last appear early in the 3rd century. Th reasons for its introduction, and for its possible passage from the cavalry in the infantry, are clear. It was much more protective than the previo legionary patterns, designed cover the soldier's whole hea against blows from long *spatha* This need was clearly felt outweigh the disadvantages of greater weight and heat, an restricted hearing (son specimens show a hole pierced the cheek-guards at ear level The original Niederbieber fir has a bronze reinforcing bar fro front to back; a bronze examp from Friedburg and iron helm from Heddernheim and Merc show a complete crucifor

Gravestone of a Roman auxiliary cavalryman from Mostar, apparently wielding a single-edged sword of Thracian type; note also the rectangular shield. See reconstruction as Plate F2. (Zemaljski Museum, Sarajevo; author's photo, courtesy the Museum)

rangement. The Osterburken helmet also had an attached frontal bar of 'iadem' shape, angled vertically (see reconstruction as Plate F4).

Among Pannonian finds one worthy of special mention is a globular onical bronze helmet of Eastern derivation now preserved in Zagreb rchaeological Museum. Attachments for missing cheek- and neck-guards e visible; an applied brow-plate is embossed with figures of Victory, piter and Mars, and the pattern of the narrow applied borders dates it the late 2nd or early 3rd century AD. Presumably belonging to some stern auxiliary unit, this is unlikely to be a product of a local workshop.

Gutter-shaped shield edging in brass, grips in iron, and boss-plates for e rectangular legionary *scutum* have been excavated at Izsa. From Sisak, ubliana and Ptuj (Poetovium) come various two-piece D-shaped bronze ickles with lily-shaped prongs, similar to those from Germania Superior. ngraved leaf-shaped 1st–2nd century AD pendants have been found at sak, and undecorated examples at Ptuj. Although most scholars associate ese pendants with horse harness, they could also be from the straps of ilitary 'aprons', or the central pieces of pendants shaped like *lunulae*. hree-leaf specimens of harness pendants come from Ljubliana and Sisak; e front of these is sometimes engraved with plant motifs and with dotted les along the edge, and a small loop at the top served to fasten them to horse *phalera*. Pickaxes have been excavated at Sisak and other camps.

ALMATIA

tes in Dalmatia have revealed a rich variety of military items. As everywhere the Empire, arrowheads are the commonest finds, and Radman-Livaja as classified seven different types from the province. Various weapon heads ite from the first two centuries of the Empire. A leaf-shaped iron example om Gardun, retaining part of the socketed shaft, measures 13.9cm by 3cm (5.5 x 1.3in) at its broadest; the shaft diameter is 1.4cm (0.55in).

Equipment fragments, 1st–2nd century AD, from Trilj (ancient Tilurium) in Dalmatia.
(1–4) Belt fittings, bronze buckles, 1st century. (5) Bronze buckle tongue, 1st century. (8) Bronze buckle with button, 1st century AD. (6, 7 & 13) Bronze buckles for laminated armour, 1st century AD. (9–11) Apron-strap fittings, bronze and silver, 1st century. (12, 16 & 17) Horse-harness pendants, second half 1st century/early 2nd century. (14, 15) Bronze mounts for reins, 1st century. (18) Bronze three-piece harness pendant, second half 1st century. (19, 20) Bronze harness pendants, 1st century. (21) Spearheads, 1st–2nd century. (22) Spear ferrule, 1st–2nd century. (23) *Dolabra*, 1st century. (Drawings by Andrea Salimbeti, ex-Ivčević)

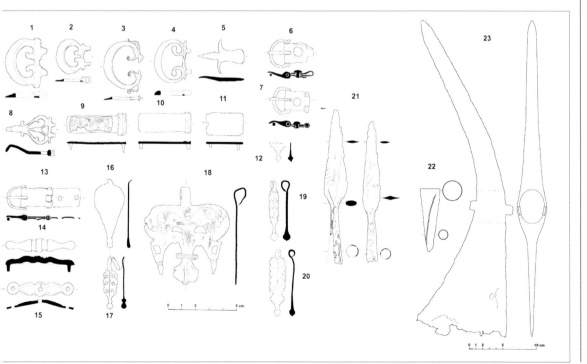

Another, with a midrib, is 20.2cm (7.9in) long and 2.1cm (0.82in) wide its broadest. A cylindrical iron butt from Trilj (Tilurium), base of Legio V Claudia Pia Fidelis, is 9.2cm (3.6in) long and 3.3cm (1.3in) wide.

From Trilj and Ivoševci we have various two-piece D-shaped bron buckles attesting the presence of laminated cuirasses in the 1st century A they are of the type now classified as Corbridge A/B and C, and th preserved mounts are identical to those found at Sisak in Pannonia. Tr has also yielded many 1st-century button-and-loop fasteners used to lir dagger or sword scabbards to belts. Bronze and silvered belt plates lil those from Germania Superior have also come to light; two silver-plate rectangular examples from Gardun are expanded and decorated wi engravings.

Horse-harness pendants and fittings from military camps date throughout the 1st century AD (e.g. Gardun, Ivoševci, Narona) are to numerous and varied to describe here in detail, but include some bron: examples whose shape and size (7cm x 6.3cm/2.75in x 2.48in) suggests u on the forehead or breast of the horse. Rather than the more usual leaf- heart-shaped pendants, rhomboid forms visible on the stele of an auxilia cavalryman from Mostar are confirmed by finds. A horse bit with trapezoid bars has also been excavated at Mostar.

Among 1st-century *dolabrae* found in the province, one from Gardun ha a head 47cm (18.5in) long, with a slightly bent pick at one end and a forge trapezoidal axe blade 13.4cm (5.3in) long at the other. The oval slot fe inserting the handle measures 5cm x 3.5cm (1.9 x 1.4in).

HISPANIA TARRACONENSIS

One of the most important military camps in this province was Aqua Querquenniae (modern Porto Quintela), station of Cohors I Gallica Civiu Romanorum Equitata, where Spanish archaeologists have recovere weapons, arrowheads, clothing items, medical instruments, tools, person belongings and pottery.

Some leaf-shaped javelin heads of rhomboidal section are 16.3cm (6.4i long – blade 9.2cm (3.6in), socket 7.1cm (2.8in) – and 2.9cm (1.1in) wic at the broadest; the round sockets are 1.5cm (0.6in) in diameter. Ferrule were also present, measuring from 4.5cm to 8.1cm (1.8–3.2in). Tw exceptional examples of the *spatha* have been dated to the 2nd centur and Monte Bernorio (Palencia) yielded fragments of Mainz-type *gladius*. Other spears (among them the *has* of a *beneficiarius*) have been found in Palencia (Lc Majuelos). The leaf shape is conventional, but example from Atebalsa (Navarra) – found together with a dagg – and from Citadela show a quadrangular section an a marked rib on the blade. A splendid scabbard an *pugio* from Palencia show that local taste still influence the production of Roman armament. Other dagge come from Cuesta del Burro (Burgos), Las Min; (Zamora), Santa Cruza de Camazos (Valladolid) an ancient Numancia.

The employment of muscle armours by senic officers is well attested by carvings in Tarraco, and als by the bronze appliqué or *cymation* from a leathe example from Palencia. *Loricae segmentatae* of Corbridg

Detail of Roman statue from Tarragona, 2nd century AD, probably representing a *praefectus alae*, a *legatus legionis* or a governor of the province. Visible on the breast is a representation of the *aegida* of the goddess Minerva. This kind of senior officers' 'muscle' armour, worn over a heavy *subarmalis* (with, though not visible here, two deep ranges of *pteryges*), suggests that the original copied by the artist was a metal *thorax statos* rather than a leather cuirass. (Museo Arqueologico de Tarragona; author's photo, courtesy of the Museum)

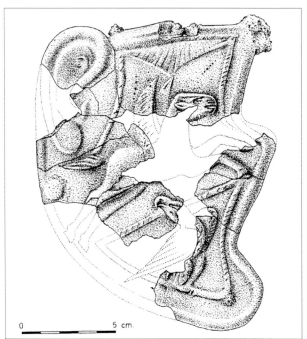

nd Newstead typology were produced in the military camp of Legio VI Victrix at Léon, over a lengthy period. Fragments of Weisenau-type helmets have been found at various camps (Herrera de Pisuerga, Porto Quintela, ruña). Petavonium (Zamora) has revealed two splendid cheek-guards, one of 2nd-century Weisenau type, and one from a 'Pseudo-Attic' helmet – probably of the new so-called Guisborough type (Robinson's Cavalry Sports Type I), so far the only example found in Spain. Two well-preserved Weisenau helmets came from a shipwreck in the Balearic Islands (Cabrera), as did a similar bronze helmet which was stolen shortly after recovery.

Small personal effects are represented by the *fibulae* of Aucissa type found at Astorga (Asturica Augusta), dated to the late 1st century BC, and others of the 1st–2nd centuries AD from Herrera de Pisuerga (base of Legio IIII Macedonica), Monte Cilda (Palencia) and Zaragoza. Belt plates decorated with niello, like examples from the northern provinces, have been found at Monte Bernorio, again associated with military brooches. Various sites have yielded hobnails from soldiers' *caligae* (military sandals), tools, and spear ferrules (El Cincho-Cantabria). Small knives for daily use were made in the same *fabrica* at Herrera de Pisuerga which produced much military equipment during the 1st and 2nd centuries: bone elements from composite bows have been found, as have horse eye-guards in bronze and leather, harness pendants, tent components, pieces of scale and laminated armours, and daggers. Fittings for *loricae segmentatae* found at Soria (San Estèban de Gormaz) are probably from the same workshop.

HISPANIA BAETICA

Finds at Cordoba include sling projectiles, catapult bolts, javelin heads, apron pendants of half-moon shape, and so on. However, the most astonishing find is the single intact Roman specimen of a bronze muscle cuirass ever discovered, recovered from a shipwreck near Cueva del Jarro (Almunécar) that is datable by its cargo of *amphorae* to the turn of the

LEFT **Iron helmet of Weisenau typology (Imperial Gallic Type A) recovered from a 1st-century AD shipwreck off Moro Boti in Hispania Tarraconensis. Note the very broad, shallow-angled neck-guard. (Drawing by Andrea Salimbeti, ex-Morillo)**

RIGHT **Decorated cheek-guard of a helmet of Guisborough typology (Robinson's Cavalry Sports Type I) from Zamora in Hispania Tarraconensis, last quarter of 2nd century AD. Note the embossed ear, and motifs of the winged horse Pegasus above an eagle. (Drawing by Andrea Salimbeti, ex-Morillo)**

Stele of Dazas, a cavalryman of _Cohors VI Delmatorum_ (Sixth Cohort of Dalmatians), 2nd century AD, from Cherchell in Mauretania Caesariensis; see reconstruction as Plate G3. (Archaeological Museum of Cherchell, Algeria; author's photo, courtesy the Museum)

1st/2nd centuries AD. The markedly muscled _stato_ approximately 40cm (15.75in) in height, may have belonged to a senior officer on the ship.

LUSITANIA

It is often difficult to ascertain the chronological contex of finds in this province. Four fragments of Weisenau-typ helmets from Conimbriga were dated to the 1st centur AD, including two rear handles from the second half o that century.

AFRICA PROCONSULARIS

No analysis has yet been made of actual finds o equipment from this province. Nevertheless, statue show plain muscle armours fitted with two or more ranges of _cymatia_ (edge lappets). A statue from Hyppe Regius, of the second half of the 2nd century AD, show shoulder-pieces and a band around the armour which are very similar to those on the monument of Favoniu Facilis from Colchester. However, while the latter probably represents leather armour the Hyppo Regiu statue seems to show a metal _statos_, worn over a _subarmalis_ fitted with a triple range of leather _pteryges_ decorated with metal elements.

MAURETANIA TINGITANA

Rich finds of various fragments of helmets, both infantry and cavalry, have been made at the military sites of Thamusida, Volubilis and Sala. Six fork shaped plume supports and one side-plume tube attest the use of at leas two different legionary helmet types: Robinson's Imperial Gallic Type C1 here dated to the 1st century BC, and the later Imperial Italic Type D. A complete iron mask helmet of AD 40–50 comes from Volubilis, and nine other fragments of these have also been found. Military camps have also revealed large numbers of spears and javelins, and harness fittings paralleling specimens from Dalmatia. Archaeology has confirmed the presence of al three main metallic body-armour types of the period: the _lorica segmentata_ scale armour, and (from Volubilis, Thamusida and Banasa) ringmail. Muscle armour is well documented in the statues of _loricati_, for example those a Caesarea. The Equites Mauri led by their prince Lusius Quietus are clearly visible on Trajan's Column, with light tunics and characteristic plaited hair They ride without saddle-cloths, and carry the _parma equestris_ shield.

MAURETANIA CAESARIENSIS

Numidian auxiliary horsemen are also represented on Trajan's Column carrying a spear and _cetra_ (buckler); they are riding bareback without ever a bridle, but simply a neck-halter. The costume of a Numidian prince o the 1st century AD, represented on a stele from Chensour, Abbassa, i substantially the same; it differs only in showing low shoes and a cloak fastened at the right shoulder, but his horse has a low saddle covered by a cloth, and some harness.

Moorish cavalrymen dressed in tunics decorated with _picti tunica Nilotid_ (Egyptian embroidery) are mentioned among escorts of the Emperor Trajan. These tunics were probably similar to those represented in some

Roman *milites* of Caesar Augustus on the march, 14 BC, in a frieze on the Arch of Segusium in the Alpes Cottiae. This is the earliest known depiction of the *lorica segmentata* on a Roman monument; the armour is probably similar to that of which fragments have been recovered from the Teutoburg Forest battlefield near Kalkriese. (Museo di Antichità, Turin; author's photo, courtesy the Museum)

osaics from Tunisia, such as the red embroidered clothing of the Muse ear Virgil, preserved in the Bardo Museum, or the long-sleeved, ulticoloured tunics of the *venatores* from Sousse.

At Tipasa four military stelae memorialize soldiers coming from various orners of the Empire: a man from Britanny with two horses, a Batavian *ntarius* lancer of the Caninefati tribe, an Iturean archer, and a spearman om central Europe. None is armoured, but their clothing, with trousers d long-sleeved tunics, anticipates that of the later Empire. In Cherchell e steles show more complete military equipment: soldiers of the Sixth ohort of Dalmatians are armed with hexagonal shields, long spears, velins, *gladius* and *pugio*, and wear scale armour over a *subarmalis* with eryges. Balaterus, of the same unit, carries not only his two javelins and learms but also a *fustis* (cudgel) for the maintenance of public order.

LPES: POENINAE, MARITIMAE & COTTIAE

om the conquests of Augustus onwards the Alpine area was strongly ilitarized. The monuments show many representations of warriors and mament, and the earliest known depiction of the *lorica segmentata* is on the nning legionaries on the Arch of Segusium (Susa). Various helmets are ulpted in detail on the funerary monument of an unknown senator of the laudian period in Augusta Taurinorum (Turin), including Buggenum-ontefortino, Attic, Coolus, Weiler, and Hellenic types.

That and other monuments show muscle armour in oth leather and metal versions. The stele of a centurion d his servant also from Turin can be dated to the Julio-laudian period by the short laminated shoulder-pieces, robably in metal, and the small rounded lappets at the wer edge. The armour is worn over a *subarmalis* fitted th two ranges of linen *pteryges* at the shoulders and one elow the waist.

ALIA

gurative representations at Pompeii and the ancelleria Relief in Rome show an interesting evolution the *pilum*: the addition, at the junction of the shank d the wooden shaft, of a bulbous weight, probably of ad, decorated with the image of an eagle. Such a

Detail of helmet of Boeotian type, from the frieze decorating the funerary monument of a senator of the Glitii family, perhaps dedicated to *Legio V Alaudae*; Claudian period, from Augusta Taurinorum (Turin) in the Alpes Cottiae. Various helmets of Hellenic typology were issued to the legions of Augustus, as clearly illustrated by monuments and by a specimen preserved in the Hamburg Museum; this is not surprising, given the amounts of booty captured in the wars against the Illyrians and Cleopatra. Note the triple crest, with central plumes and side feathers. (Museum of Antiquities, Turin; author's photo, courtesy the Museum)

Panoply of a Roman cavalryman, from a painted stucco relief in a 1st-century AD necropolis in Pompeii, here in a 19th-century drawing from the original. The spear has a broad, ribbed, leaf-shaped blade (perhaps with a weight at the socket?) and a metal ferrule. The Mainz-type sword and the dagger are worn on separate belts; note the free ends divided into three studded straps – the origin of the Roman soldier's famous 'apron' hanging over the groin. The sword has a white hilt and a bronze-framed scabbard painted red; despite the decay of the past century, traces of red paint can still be seen today. The dagger has a bronze hilt and a bronze-decorated iron scabbard. The *clipeus* or *parma equestris* shield is painted black (outer, with a 'wreathed grass' effect) and red, with an embossed bronze head of Medusa as the *umbo*. (Courtesy Soprintendenza Archeologica dei beni culturali di Pompeii, Herculaneum & Stabia)

weight would increase the penetrative power of the weapon, but this kind of *pilum* may have been reserved to the Praetorian Guard or other elite units serving in Italy.

Helmets of Praetoriani, Urbaniciani and Vigiles are represented decorated with high plumes of feathers or hair, often, as in the Pompeian frescoes, coloured red. Flaccus (*Argonautica*, III, 176) describes a helmet with *cristae rubentes* (red plumes). A mention by Tacitus (*Hist.*, 1, 38) of an episode during the civil war tells us that auxiliary, legionary and Praetorian units were distinguished by their *insignia*; most scholars misinterpret this term, but Tacitus' addition of the words '*galeis scutisque*' clearly shows that in this case *insignia*, used in the plural, means both helmet crests and shield blazons. Again, the fact that shield blazons identified units is confirmed by Tacitus's story of two Praetorians picking up enemy shields from the ground and infiltrating through their ranks. These elements sometimes help us to distinguish the various corps depicted on Roman monuments, where the kind of armour worn is not a definitive identification. On military gravestones of the first two centuries of the Empire the dress of the deceased legionaries and auxiliaries is indistinguishable, but in some cases shield blazons or unit standards can be associated with the units named in the inscriptions.

The Ninth Praetorian Cohort, the only one attested in the Dacian campaigns, is identified on Trajan's Column by the *signa* adorned with imperial *imagines*, as also depicted on the late 1st-century tombstone from Tusculum of the *centurio* Pompeus Asper of the Third Praetorian Cohort. Other identifying elements are the crests shown on representations of Imperial Gallic and Imperial Italic helmets, all of these subjects wearing laminated armour.

Although decreasing in favour of iron specimens, the production of bronze helmets according to the Italic tradition lasted until the late 1st century AD, as attested by the Buggenum-Montefortino specimen found on the Bedriacum battlefield. The Attic specimens from Pompeii were probably reserved for the Urban Cohorts in the city, but this helmet, with its deep, decorated frontal, is often represented on the heads of guardsmen in sculpted Italian monuments of the 1st and 2nd centuries.

The surface of cavalry shields might be lavishly painted and/or decorated with appliqués. At Pompeii painted stucco reliefs in the tomb of a cavalryman, today greatly deteriorated, were still visible in their original colours at the beginning of the 20th century. They represented his panoply of arms: spears, sword, dagger and shield (see accompanying photo). The partly black-painted shield echoes a description of Jupiter *nigrans clipeus* by the poet Flaccus (*Argonautica*, VIII, 354–355).

SICILIA, SARDINIA and CORSICA

Portovecchio in Corsica has yielded the earliest specimen yet found of the Pompeii-type *gladius*, and its wood and bronze scabbard has been restored by the Laboratoire du Centre des Recherches et d'ètudes Archéologiques de Vienne. It shows the passage from the Mainz to the Pompeii types in have been progressive during the 1st century AD, but the construction of the scabbard now seems to have become a simple assembly of metal parts. A mosaic with shields representing the blazons of the Vigiles, from the area of Sassari in Sardinia, and fragments of statues of *loricati*, suggest that the equipment of Italian troops sent to patrol Sardinia in the Emperor's name was as rich as would be expected.

SELECT BIBLIOGRAPHY

Note: For reasons of space, we can list here only the ancient sources and a handful of the standard modern works. A much fuller bibliography of the relevant academic publications, in several languages, can be found on the Osprey website, by following: www.ospreypublishing.com/maa_506_bibliography

Ancient sources

Aulus Gellius (Aul. Gell.), *Attic Nights – Noctes Atticae* (*Noct. Att.*); Latin text & English translated by J.C. Rolfe in Aulus Gellius: *Attic Nights*, Vol III, Books 14–20 (Loeb Classical Library; London, 1927)

Caesar (Caes.), *The Wars (Commentaries on the Gallic War – De Bello Gallico* (*BG*); Latin text in *Commentarii de Bello Gallico*, ed. Otto Seel (Leipzig, 1961); English text in *De Bello Gallico & Other Commentaries*, trans. W.A. MacDevitt (London & Toronto, 1940)

Cassius Dio, *Roman History – Romaika* (*Rom.*); Greek & English text in Loeb Classical Library, 9 vols (Harvard University Press, 1914–1927)

Isidorus of Seville (Is.), *Etymologiae* (*Et.*); Latin text in *Isidori Hispanensis Episcopi Etymologiarum sive Originum Libri XX*, ed.W.M. Lindsay I–II (Oxford, 1911, available online at <http://en.wikipedia.org/wiki/Etymologiae>)

Pliny the Elder, *Natural History – Historia Naturalis* (*HN*); Latin & English text in Loeb Classical Library, *Pliny (the Elder). Natural History*, 10 vols (Harvard University Press, 1938–1962)

Propertius (Prop.), *The Elegies – Elegiae* (*El.*); Latin & English text in Loeb Classical Library, *Propertius, Elegies* (Harvard University Press, 1990)

Pseudo-Hyginus (Pseudo-Hyg.), *The Fortifications of the Camp – De Munitionibus Castrorum* (*De Mun. Castr.*); Latin & English text in C.M. Gilliver, 'The *de munitionibus castrorum*: Text and Translation', *Journal of Roman Military Equipment Studies* (Volume 4, 1993) pp. 33–48

Scriptores Historiae Augustae (*SHA*), Latin and English text in *Historia Augusta*, 3 vols, Loeb Classical Library (Harvard University Press, 1921–1932)

Tacitus (Tac.), *Annals – Annales* (*Ann.*); Latin & English text in *Tacitus IV, Annals 4–6, 11–12*, and *Tacitus V, Annals 4–6, 13–16*, Loeb Classical Library (Harvard University Press, 1937)

Tacitus, *The Histories – Historiae* (*Hist.*); *Tacitus II, Histories 1–3*, trans. C.H. Moore, Loeb Classical Library (Harvard University Press, 1925); *Tacitus III, Histories 4–5, Annals 1–3*, Loeb Classical Library (Harvard University Press, 1931)

Valerius Flaccus, *Argonautica*; Latin & English text in *Argonautica*, Valerius Flaccus, Loeb Classical Library (Harvard University Press, 1934)

Virgil, II, *Aeneid-Appendix Vergiliana*, Loeb Classical Library (Harvard University Press, 1918)

Modern works

Bishop, M.C. & J.C.N. Coulston, *Roman Military Equipment, From the Punic Wars to the Fall of Rome* (London, 1993 & Oxford, 2006)

D'Amato, R., *Arms and Armour of the Imperial Roman Soldier, from Marius to Commodus, 112 BC-192 AD* (London, 2009)

Dixon, K.R. & P. Southern, *The Roman Cavalry, from the First to the Third Century AD* (London, 1992)

Haynes, I., *Blood of the Provinces, the Roman Auxilia and the making of Provincial Society from Augustus to the Severans* (Oxford, 2013)

Holder, P.A., *The Roman Army in Britain* (London, 1982)

Robinson, H.R., *The Armour of Imperial Rome* (London, 1975)

Robinson, H.R., *What the Soldiers Wore on Hadrian's Wall* (Newcastle upon Tyne, 1976)

1st-century AD *gladius* scabbard of Pompeii type, from Portovecchio, Corsica. (Drawing by Andrea Salimbeti, ex-Feugère)

PLATE COMMENTARIES

A: THE GALLIC PROVINCES

1: Gallo-Roman cavalry officer; Narbonensis, late 1st century BC/early 1st century AD

Copied from the statue of a warrior from Vachères in Haute Provence dating from the Augustan period, this figure represents the high-quality equipment of Romanized Celtic aristocrats serving in the *auxilia*, as also confirmed by the richness of their grave goods (e.g. the Tiberian/Caligulan example from Chassenard). The gold *torques* around his neck shows that such leaders preserved their social status after their incorporation into the Roman world. The most costly element of his panoply, the long-sleeved shirt of *Gallica* (ringmail), has doubled *humeralia* (shoulder-guards) lined with leather and fastened with hooks on the breast. His helmet is of the Agen-Port typology, based on various finds from Alesia and elsewhere in Gaul. The shield, damaged in the original sculpture, has been reconstructed as being of hexagonal shape. Obscured at this angle is a long sword of La Tene 3 typology, similar to those found at Alesia, but now worn suspended not from a waist chain but from a Roman-style belt.

2: Auxiliary, *Cohors Mediolanensis*; Aquitania, first half of 1st century AD

Based upon aspects of the Mediolanum relief, he wears an iron and bronze Weiler-type helmet as usually shown in a cavalry context, but also a *lorica segmentata* of Kalkriese typology. He is equipped with items suggested by finds at the nearby camp of Aunedonnacum: a convex rectangular shield, and a short *hasta* spear. The long Roman-style sword, copied from a Giubiasco grave find, may be typical of Celtic auxiliaries. We show him wearing Gallic trousers beneath a Roman tunic of unbleached wool decorated with *clavi*.

3: Auxiliary cavalryman of a *Cohors Torquata*; Mediolanum, Aquitania, early 2nd century AD

Reconstructed after a sculpture now in the Archaeological Museum at Saintes, this too suggests the equipment of an aristocratic Gallo-Roman cavalryman. Note the combination of a Roman *lorica squamata*, with an applied *gorgoneion* (Gorgon's head) on the breast, and a Gallic *torques*. The highly embossed helmet of bi-metal construction has elements in common with a recent find from the Iron Gates in present-day Serbia; we have given it a tall crest and side-plumes in the yellow described by Arrian for 2nd-century cavalrymen.

4: Auxiliary cavalryman; Arlon, Belgica, AD 161–180

The relief from Arlon (see title page of this book) clearly shows the shoulder-guards of the laminated iron *lorica segmentata* – traditionally associated by scholars with legionaries or praetorians – being worn by cavalrymen over mail or perhaps leather armour. It is becoming ever clearer that this mass-produced, economic and effective defence was also issued to some auxiliary units. We should bear in mind that the ringmail which scholars have traditionally ascribed to the *auxilia* took much more time to manufacture, and would have been significantly costly. Again, this trooper wears a Weiler-type helmet.

B: THE GERMANIC PROVINCES

1: Caius Marius, legionary cavalryman, *Legio I Germanica*; Bonna, Germania Inferior, AD 40

This legionary horseman's stele identifies him as being from the Voltinii tribe. He is shown bareheaded, and wearing over his *corium* (leather corselet) the *dona militaria* he has earned by his bravery: two *armillae* and nine *phalerae*. His shield is of the Celtic hexagonal shape, and he carries a *venabulum* (short javelin); his footwear are closed *calcei* shoes. This legion was disbanded in c.AD 70 after the mutinies in Germany led by Julius Civilis against Vespasian's accession.

2: Firmus, auxiliary infantryman, *Cohors Raetorum*; Antunacum, Germania Superior, first half 1st century AD

This Raetian auxiliary is copied from his stele, where he is shown armed with two javelins and clad in a leather corselet worn over a *thorax laneus*; note too his bracelets, apparently characteristic of Raetians. Over his head and shoulders he is wearing a *paenula*. The colours for the reconstruction have been copied from those proposed by archaeologists and from the tombstone of the cavalryman Silius of Ala Picentiana, which were still visible in the 19th century. His sidearms, a *gladius* of Mainz typology and a *pugio*, are worn on the crossed belts typical of the period. During the Tiberian period the Celtic fashion for cutting the free end of a waist belt into three hanging strips had begun to evolve into the separate 'apron' of studded straps protecting the groin and thighs, always terminating in pendants. The mounts might be silvered and sometimes decorated, with plant motifs, bosses bearing imperial images, or even inscriptions. The rattle and glitter of the apron must have contributed to the impressive appearance of Roman units on the march. Only the infantry wore them; they fell into disuse during the reign of Septimius Severus, when monuments show their last representations.

3: Legionary, *Legio XI Claudia*; Vindonissa, Germania Superior, AD 100

This legionary is based on Trajan's Column and on finds at Vindonissa. His helmet is of Weisenau (Imperial Gallic) type; he wears the complex articulated *lorica segmentata* of what modern scholars term Corbridge Type A, over a long-sleeved leather *subarmalis*. His *gladius* of the new Pompeii typology is suspended by a baldric, and an apron of studded straps hangs from his dagger belt. His main weapon is a *pilum*, which can be reconstructed with confidence from the many recovered remnants. Various examples of leather shield covers have been found, complete with the identifying *tabulae ansatae*, on the Vindonissa site.

4: Legionary cavalryman, *Legio VIIII (IX) Hispana*, dressed for Hippika Gymnasia; Noviomagus, Germania Inferior, AD 120–131

The splendid equipment for the cavalry 'sports', a competitive display of the horse-soldier's skills, includes a silvered mask helmet, leg armour, and a 'Cimmerian' tunic here copied from the fresco in the Capua Mythraeum. His horse harness includes a plated chamfron, and numerous silvered *phalerae* suspended from the straps. See also Plate C2.

C: BRITANNIA

1: *Signifer, Ala Augusta Gallorum Petriana Milliaria Civium Romanorum*; Corstopitum, late 1st century AD

From the gravestone of Longinus, now at Hexham Abbey, this auxiliary cavalry standard-bearer wears a mask helmet with a high crest and pairs of tall feathers at the sides. He is armoured with ringmail worn over a *subarmalis* and a tunic of local weave; note, again, a Gallic torque round his neck. His oval shield is slung; he carries a standard of this Gallic regiment representing the *Sol Invictus*.

Detail of stele of a cavalryman, 1st–2nd century AD, now in Worms Museum. The helmet of Weiler typology (Robinson's Auxiliary Cavalry Type I) shows hair-effect embossing on the bowl, a decorated brow band rising to a point at the front, and a broad decorated cheek-guard; note the pronounced carving of the ear. (Photo courtesy Dr Stefano Izzo)

Legionary from Trajan's Column, fighting with a spear during the Dacian Wars. A small Capricorn can be made out incised on the shield boss, suggesting identification of this soldier as a member of *Legio I Minervia* from Germania Inferior, whose *signum* is also depicted in the frieze close to this figure. (Scene XCVI of cast in Museo della Civiltà Romana, Rome; author's photo, courtesy the Museum)

2: Sextus Valerius Genialis, *Ala Augusta Vocontiorum Civium Romanorum*, dressed for Hippika Gymnasia; Corinium, 1st–2nd century AD

Besides more conventional specimens and fragments of Imperial Gallic and Imperial Italic helmets, Britain has yielded precious examples of mask helmets, especially from Newstead in Scotland. Two large 1st-century helmets are made of brass (bright yellow copper alloy), and of iron; the iron example, though damaged, retains its mask, and a third female mask was also found. The stele of Genialis, from Cirencester, suggests that such helmets were worn not only for the Hippika Gymnasia but also in battle; we reconstruct his helmet from the copper-alloy bowl and the iron mask from Newstead. His composite armour is made from layered, glued linen, with iron shoulder plates and a decorative copper-alloy breastplate featuring a Gorgon's head.

3: Legionary, *Legio II Augusta*; Isca Silurum, Hadrianic period

The legionary is reconstructed according to finds made at his legion's fortress at Caerleon, including his laminated *lorica* of Newstead typology, though his Imperial Gallic helmet is copied from the Brigetio specimen from Pannonia. His shield is decorated with the Capricorn *deigmaton* displayed by this legion from the reign of Augustus. By the Hadrianic period it had been stationed in western Britannia for about three military generations, and we have included Celtic elements in his clothing. As well as *bracae* his legs are protected by *tibiales* leggings, and the old *caligae* sandals have now given way to closed *calcei* shoes.

4: Legionary cavalryman, *Legio II Augusta*; Antonine Wall, mid-2nd century AD

The stele upon which we base this figure shows a face-enclosing helmet of the new Heddernheim typology (Robinson's Auxiliary Cavalry Type E), and a muscled cuirass which must have been made of hardened leather. The reign of Antoninus Pius saw the first examples of this very different type of sword baldric. Note the employment of a javelin and of a small oval shield, the latter perhaps captured from Celtic enemies?

D: RAETIA, NORICUM & ALPES

1: Auxiliary infantryman of the *Lepontii*; Raetia, Augustan period

Graves at Giubiasco give us good archaeological evidence for the early *auxilia* recruited among Celtic Alpine peoples for the army of Augustus, including the spear, sword and scabbard, and Celtic shield with an *umbo* applied over its central reinforcing keel. The bronze helmet is of Negau Alpine typology of the Castiel group.

2: Titus Exomnius Mansuetus, *Praefectus, Cohors II Hispanorum*; Sedunum, Raetia, Flavian period

The gravestone of T. Exomnius Mansuetus from his unit's station at Sedunum (Sion) is a rare representation of a prefect in his armour. The commander of the Second Cohort of Spaniards was of equestrian rank. Despite damage to the stele it is clear that he wears a muscle cuirass over a *subarmalis* fitted with *pteryges* at shoulders and waist. Fastened at his right shoulder, with the usual circular type of *fibula*, is the *paludamentum* campaign cloak of senior officers, extending down to the calf and usually of red colour. We have chosen to show Exomnius armed with a short Greek-style sword, the so-called *parazonium*, reserved for emperors,

45

generals, officers and guardsmen, and worn on the left side by means of a baldric. Widely attested in the iconography, its bronze hilt was often shaped like an eagle's head, above a rectangular crossguard following ancient models.

3: Auxiliary infantryman, *Cohors II Raetorum*; Raetia, AD 107–166
We base this auxiliary partly upon Trajan's Column and partly upon finds at Aalen fort, which are a mine of information for the equipment of the soldiers on the Limes Raeticus. Under his *paenula* cloak he wears a ringmail shirt over a leather corselet with a dagged hem, and his bronze helmet follows Robinson's reconstructed Auxiliary Infantry Type C, with vertical cruciform reinforcing bars.

4: Legionary cavalryman, *Legio II Pia Italica*; Juvavum, Noricum, Antonine period
This man's basic equipment is taken from Marcus Aurelius's Column and finds made in this province. His helmet is based on the Imperial Italic example from Theilenhofen, which had an applied bronze brow band and cruciform reinforcement bars. Note the new method of attaching the *spatha* scabbard to the baldric, with an external loop or bracket. Horse-harness mounts similar to examples from Germania Superior and Dalmatia have been excavated at Juvavum (Salzburg),

E: THE HISPANIC PROVINCES

1: Legionary, *Legio IIII Macedonica*; Hispania Tarraconensis, first half of 1st century AD
This man is armed with finds from the camp at Herrera de Pisuerga. Copying a mosaic from this province, he wears a *lorica segmentata* (here hidden under his *paenula* cloak) in combination with a Pseudo-Attic helmet of which fragments have been found at Zamora.

2: *Centurio Primipilus* Marcus Vettius Valens, *Legio VI Victrix Hispaniensis*; Lusitania, AD 68
This magnificent veteran officer wears a Weisenau-type helmet copied from fragments found at Conimbriga; the bronze brow band has incised decorations filled with black niello. Note his leather muscle armour, worn over a *subarmalis* fitted with ranges of linen *pteryges,* and the polished bronze greaves copied from a rare Spanish find at Merida. The most immediately impressive feature is the highly decorative set of *dona militaria* – two *torques* and nine *phalerae* – worn on a strap harness over his armour. As a centurion he wears his *gladius* on the left hip slung from a baldric, but his expensively decorated dagger is fastened to a conventional plated *cingulum* belt. He carries both the vine staff symbolic of his rank, and a weighted *pilum*.

3: *Praefectus, Ala II Flavia Hispaniorum Civium Romanorum*; Petavonium, Hispania Tarraconensis, 2nd century AD
The finds made in this province include a great deal of horse equipment, attesting to the local importance of cavalry. Fragments of Pseudo-Attic helmets allow us to reconstruct a rich example for this unit commander of the equestrian order, clad in a leather muscled *thorax studios* decorated with the *aegis* of the goddess Minerva. This and a *parazonium* sword are almost hidden by a red-fringed white *lacerna* cloak. Other marks of senior rank are the carefully knotted red sash *(zona militaris* or *cinctorium)*, and the Greek-type *phaecasia* boots.

4: Auxiliary *cornicularius, Cohors V Baetica*; Ilipula Minor, Hispania Baetica, 2nd century AD
The rank of this man is indicated by his elaborately embossed helmet, reconstructed from a sculpture now in the Museum of Grenada. A fresco from this province shows a military man ou hunting, clad in an off-white tunic decorated with *clavi*; and small statuette shows the employment of shields of Doncaste typology.

F: PANNONIA & DALMATIA

1: Caius Castricius Victor, *Legio II Adiutrix*; Aquincum, Pannonia Inferior, AD 88–92
Reconstructed largely from his stele, this legionary wears bronze helmet of Imperial Gallic Type H similar to a specime now in the Germanisches Nationalmuseum, Nuremberg; her we interpret the side ornaments not as feather plumes, bu as horns indicating the status of *cornicularius*. We interpre his armour as a leather corselet with three ranges of *pteryge* below the waist, and an apron of studded straps hangin from his dagger belt. Swords might still be hung from a wais belt or, as here, a baldric; bronze or silvered decorativ bosses impressed with an imperial image are typical of find from Aquincum and Siscia. The oval legionary shield show a Gorgon's-head boss and applied copper-alloy lightnin bolts.

2: Thracian auxiliary cavalryman; Mostar area, Dalmatia, 1st century AD
This cavalryman is copied from his stele; he seems to wea an Attic style of Imperial Italic helmet, and to carry

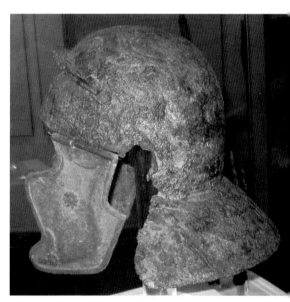

Iron legionary helmet of Imperial Gallic typology from Brigetio in Pannonia, 2nd century AD. Robinson suggests a date of AD 100–125 for this helmet, which has a much large neck-guard than his Types G, H and I, sloping steeply down toward the shoulders at an angle of nearly 45 degrees. The bronze ornaments are in the usual places for this category o helmets, except on the cheek-guards, where only two rosettes were used – one at the centre of the plate, and the other over the rivet holding the chin-lace tie-ring inside. It formerly had an applied bronze brow band, and another bronze strip on the forward edge of the reinforcing 'peak'; the 'eyebrows' are very broad and flat, with a medial step, and were placed high on the front of the bowl. For a reconstruction, see Plate C3. (Caerleon Museum; photo courtesy Dr Cezary Wyszynski)

gle-edged sword. His shield is identical in size and shape that found at Doncaster, England.

Legionary of a *vexillatio, Legio IIII Flavia Felix;* rmium, Trajanic period
is reconstruction of a soldier carrying his *sarcina* (camping uipment) on the march lashed to a *furca* (forked pole) is m Trajan's Column, where the original source shows the iployment of up to three waist belts by one legionary. The ts, worn over the armour, had a dual purpose: to transfer iart of the weight of the armour from the soldier's shoulders his hips, and to support the sword and dagger, purses and ier accoutrements. The armour illustrated is of Newstead/ irnuntum type.

***Optio* Aelius Septimus, *Legio II Adiutrix;* iuincum, end of 2nd century AD**
judge from his stele, this *optio* of the period of the ircomannic Wars is clad in a leather muscle armour, which m this period onwards began to be used not only by icers but also by junior ranks. The armour is decorated cording to the style seen in the Germanic provinces. The ilmet is of the new Niederbieber typology, with massive, nged face-guards and an upturned frontal 'peak'. His ierary stele shows a wide baldric, a waist belt introducing e ring-fastening system familiar in the 3rd century, and a iver of light javelins.

THE AFRICAN PROVINCES

Auxiliary cavalryman, *Ala I Augusta Gallorum*, essed for Hippika Gymnasia; Volubilis, iauretania Tingitana, AD 40
Africa, as elsewhere, splendid accoutrements were used the Hippika Gymnasia 'tournaments'. The highly decorated mmerian' *bracae pictae* (tunic and trousers) are copied m a North African coloured mosaic showing Virgil and the ises now in the Bardo Museum, Tunis. The helmet mask is :onstructed from one found at Volubilis, of iron covered h silvered bronze; it had an internal leather lining to protect e face, which must have been a general practice.

Auxiliary *signifer, Cohors III Asturum Civium imanorum*; Mauretania Tingitana, AD 86
is standard-bearer, from the famous Pintaius stele, is itinguished by a bearskin worn over his bronze helmet and ither corselet. Splendid examples of military belts have en recovered from Roman fort sites; they were a proud sign the military calling, and in Africa, as elsewhere, legionaries d men of auxiliary cohorts wore both sword and dagger ts. Probably for practical reasons, given the burden of ndling the standard, this *signifer* wears his sidearms in the infiguration seen on centurions' monuments, with the idius on the left and the *pugio* on the right.

Dazas, auxiliary cavalryman, *Cohors VI ilmatarum*; Mauretania Caesariensis, AD 107
constructed mainly from his funerary stele, this Dalmatian valryman carries a javelin and a hexagonal shield; the izon is copied from a miniature shield on which a Dalmatian igmaton survives. The stele of Dazas son of Scenus (see ge 40) seems to depict him bareheaded, but the use of iirygian' caps and helmets is attested by statuettes from s area. There have also been many finds of *squamae* from ale armours, as shown on the stele with some kind of plain nds passing over the shoulders. Boots, of Egyptian iology, begin to appear on representations of cavalrymen this period.

4: Auxiliary lancer, *Ala I Caninafatium*; Mauretania Caesariensis, Antonine period
This figure is reconstructed from the stele of Tipasa, an *auditor* in this unit. The long cavalry *contus* lance was used with both hands. The trooper is not armoured; it is on monuments in the African provinces that we first see the major contemporary changes in Roman military clothing – a long-sleeved tunic decorated with *clavi*, trousers and boots.

H: ITALIA

1: Legionary, *Legio I Adiutrix*; Rome, AD 68
This man, taken from the Mainz Column, is equipped with elements found at Aquileia: the Imperial Gallic helmet, the *lorica segmentata* with the particular hinges found there, and other equipment typical of the second half of the 1st century AD, like the rectangular semi-cylindrical shield and the *pilum*. The *lorica* plate fastening arrangement represented here is a hypothetical reconstruction of one of many examples from Trajan's Column, with a buckled strap fastening the upper breast plates. This legion, recruited from a Legio I Classica, supported the causes of first Galba and then Otho during the 'Year of the Four Emperors'; it was then sent north by Vitellius to put down the Batavian rebellion.

2: *Beneficiarius*, Praetorian Guard, AD 90
This picked soldier wears a heavily embossed Pseudo-Attic helmet with a deep 'triangular' frontal feature above a brow band, and a *lorica segmentata* of Corbridge typology. The *hasta* spear with the elaborate head that distinguishes his status of 'beneficiary' is copied, like the embossed *clipeus* shield, from the Cancelleria Relief and from the sculptures of the Templum Gentis Flaviae.

3: *Eques Singularis Augusti*, Hadrianic period
The appearance of this young Greek of the Imperial Horseguards echoes, probably deliberately, that associated with the entourage of Alexander the Great, who was depicted using a panther-skin saddle cloth. He is dressed in a scale armour fitted with *humeralia*, according to the old fashion. His Attic helmet is splendidly embossed and has an animal crest; his *cothurni* (high boots) are also borrowed from the Greek world.

1st-century AD helmet of Weisenau type, of the pattern classified by Robinson as Imperial Gallic Type D – although this specimen was found near Aquileia, the major arms manufacturing centre in X Regio of Italia. It shows extensive yellow-metal fittings, and red insets on the ornamental rosettes. (Museo Archeologico Nazionale, Aquileia, courtesy Ministero per i beni e le attività culturali; author's photo)

INDEX

References to illustration captions are shown in **bold**. Plates are shown with page and caption locators in brackets.